The
5-Minute
BIBLE
STUDY
for Men

ISBN 978-1-64352-274-6

Some content in this book has been abridged from previous writings by the same author.

Published by Barbour Books, an imprint of Barbour Publishing, Inc., 1810 Barbour Drive, Uhrichsville, Ohio 44683, www.barbourbooks.com

Our mission is to inspire the world with the life-changing message of the Bible.

Member of the
Evangelical Christian
Publishers Association

Printed in the United States of America.

The
5-Minute
BIBLE
STUDY
for Men

David Sanford

BARBOUR BOOKS
An Imprint of Barbour Publishing, Inc.

Introduction

Do you find it hard to make time for Bible study? You intend to do it but the hours turn into days, and before you know it, another week has passed and you have not picked up God's Word. This book provides an avenue for you to open the Bible regularly and dig into a passage—even if you only have five minutes!

Minutes 1–2: **Read** carefully the scripture passage for each day's Bible study.

Minute 3: **Understand.** Ponder a couple of prompts designed to help you apply the verses from the Bible to your own life. Consider these throughout your day as well.

Minute 4: **Apply.** Read a reflection based on the day's scriptural focus. Think about what you are learning and how to apply these truths to your own life.

Minute 5: **Pray.** A prayer starter will help you to begin a time of conversation with God. Remember to allow time for Him to speak into your life as well.

May *The 5-Minute Bible Study for Men* help you to establish the discipline of studying God's Word. Head out to your car or truck five minutes early with this book and your Bible. Your willingness to spend these minutes focused on God's Word and prayer can make a huge difference in your day!

Start by Saying "Thank You!"
Read 1 Thessalonians 5:12–24

Key Verse:

*Give thanks in all circumstances; for this is
the will of God in Christ Jesus for you.*
1 THESSALONIANS 5:18 ESV

Understand:

- *What do you hope to get out of this book?*
- *Among other things, would you like to
  gain a better understanding of how to
  read and study the Bible?*

Apply:

Imagine you're sitting in your truck beginning your
very first Bible study in this book. Remember how
you felt when you first bought the truck? It's not the
truck of your dreams, and you can't forget the disap-
pointment of that first dent, but it's served you well.
Even the tear in the passenger seat says, in effect, *This
is my truck.*

As you turn to look at that tear, you remember
who always rides along with you. Imagine giving
Him your Bible, turned to the page(s) for today's
reading, and asking the Lord, "Would You please
read this to me? And would You please speak today's

key verse straight to my heart?" Jesus smiles of course, and says yes.

Today is a great day to say thank you to the mentor, friend, or family member who gave you this *5-Minute Bible Study for Men* book. It's also a great day to say thanks to the Lord, who wants to fortify, strengthen, and encourage you as you go through each Bible study over the next three months.

Pray:

Yes, Lord, I want to say "Thank You!" Please fortify, strengthen, and encourage me today.

Saying "Wow!"
Read Psalm 8:1–9

Key Verse:

O LORD, our Lord, your majestic name fills the earth!
PSALM 8:1 NLT

Understand:

- *Where are some of the most picturesque places you've ever been?*
- *Where are two or three of your all-time favorite places to visit?*

Apply:

Imagine today that you have to drive quite a ways into the countryside. You can't help feeling nostalgic about some of the most beautiful places you'll pass along the way. Seeing a strikingly beautiful place for the first time stirs feelings of transcendence, of "Wow!"

Conversely, spoiled creation produces embarrassment or disgust at the wasteful, sinful actions of other men. Yet many awe-inspiring places still remain. Each place speaks to you in a deep and mysterious way. Often, it's the Holy Spirit inside you, lifting your heart with a fresh revelation of the Lord God's infinite, eternal power and glory.

True, creation can't tell us everything about God,

but what it says is of first importance. The Lord God could but speak the word and create the entire universe. And, yes, He made you, planted the seed of faith in your heart, helped you understand the Good News of Jesus Christ, and is at work in your heart and life to this day.

Saying "Wow!" when you see the marvels of creation is important because it draws your heart closer to God. May you experience "Wow!" even more frequently as you see amazing, God-inspired truths in scripture during these next three months.

Along the way, you'll have opportunities to say "Wow!" to God's inspiration of the Bible, preservation of the scriptures, the miracle of translation, and much more.

Pray:

Yes, Lord, I want to say "Wow!" for Your majestic name! I also want to say "Wow!" for all You have in store for me as I read Your Word. Please keep changing me from the inside out.

Why the Bible Is Inspired by God
Read Psalm 119:1–24

Key Verse:

*Open my eyes, that I may behold
wondrous things out of your law.*
PSALM 119:18 ESV

Understand:

- *What does it look like when a creative
  person is inspired?*
- *What did it look like when God inspired
  the biblical writers? Any guesses?*

Apply:

When you decide to study the Bible, you want to know
for certain that it's inspired by God, not mere mortals.
Here are four compelling reasons to say "Wow!"

1. Scripture is consistently called "the Word of God."
Psalm 119 best demonstrates this by using ten different terms for God's Word. What's more, the prophets indirectly identify their writings as God's Word
by using introductory phrases such as "The LORD
said to me" and "The word of the LORD came to. . . ."
The authors knew they were speaking God's words
(Deuteronomy 18:15–22 and Jeremiah 36:27).

2. Scripture states directly that it is inspired by

God. Second Timothy 3:16 uses the word *inspiration* (*God-breathed* in the New International Version), and other passages strongly support this truth. Second Peter 1:20–21 teaches that men "moved" ("carried along" in the NIV) by the Holy Spirit wrote scripture. Jesus and Peter said inspiration is God choosing to communicate *His* message through *men* (Mark 12:36, Acts 4:25, and 2 Peter 1:21).

3. *Scripture is spoken of as if it were God.* See Galatians 3:8 and Genesis 12:1–3. Conversely, God is spoken of as if He is scripture (Hebrews 3:7 with Psalm 95:7). This shows the close, intimate connection between God and His Word.

4. *Old Testament authors recognized God as their source.* Moses told the people of Israel that what he had commanded them was from the Lord God (Deuteronomy 4:2). In 2 Samuel 23:2, King David on his deathbed stated that the Spirit of the Lord had spoken through him.

There's more!

Pray:

*Yes, Lord, I want to say "Wow!" for inspiring
every page in my Bible. I'm so glad
I can read it with confidence.*

More Reasons Why the Bible Is Inspired
Read Mark 12:18–37

Key Verse:

Jesus replied, "Are you not in error because you do not know the Scriptures or the power of God?"
MARK 12:24 NIV

Understand:

- *Humanly speaking, who is the most creative, artistic, and inspired person you know?*
- *To what degree do you think the Bible is inspired by God? Books? Chapters? Verses? Words?*

Apply:

You can know for certain that the Bible is divinely inspired for two more compelling reasons:

5. *Jesus Christ fully supported all of scripture.* See Matthew 5:17–19. He confirmed its historical accuracy, down to the tense of a verb (Mark 12:26). He declared that scripture is permanent (Matthew 5:17–18), is inspired by the Holy Spirit (Mark 12:36), contains enough information to support our faith (Luke 16:29–31), is unbreakable (John 10:35),

and agrees with His teachings (John 5:46–47 and Luke 24:27, 44).

6. *The New Testament writers viewed both testaments as the Word of God.* Peter affirmed that the Holy Spirit inspired the Old Testament (Acts 4:25). He compared the commandments of Jesus Christ, which the apostles taught, with the words the holy prophets spoke (2 Peter 3:2). He declared that the Gospel that was preached to them was the Word of the Lord (1 Peter 1:23, 25). Peter also recognized Paul's writings as part of scripture (2 Peter 3:15–16).

The apostle Paul confirmed that the Old Testament is accurate in its historical details (1 Corinthians 10:1–11). Paul cited the Old Testament and Gospels as scripture (1 Thessalonians 5:18). He went on to state forcefully that he preached God's Word, not his own message (1 Thessalonians 2:13). The New Testament authors knew that God had entrusted them with His Word (1 Timothy 4:1–3, Titus 1:3, and Revelation 1:1–3). Wow, indeed!

Pray:

Yes, Lord, I want to say "Thank You!" for these further proofs that You inspired every page in my Bible. I can call it God's Word knowing that's exactly what it is.

Your Response to Scripture
Read Daniel 9:1–19

Key Verse:

*I, Daniel, learned from reading the word of the LORD,
as revealed to Jeremiah the prophet, that Jerusalem
must lie desolate for seventy years. So I turned to the
Lord God and pleaded with him in prayer and fasting.*
DANIEL 9:2–3 NLT

Understand:

- *How easy or difficult is it for you to take
  God at His word?*
- *What would make it easier for you?*

Apply:

Do you remember who always rides along with you?
Imagine asking the Lord, "Would you please read
today's passage to me?" Jesus smiles and says yes.
When He finishes, He doesn't close your Bible and
give it back to you. Instead, He looks back at you and
smiles again.

You wait expectantly, but the Lord doesn't say
anything. Then it occurs to you, *Oh, He wants* me *to
say something. He wants to know my response to what
He just spoke to my heart.*

The easiest response is to pray: "Lord, I thank

You for Daniel 9:2–3, which says, 'I, Daniel, learned from reading the word of the LORD. . . .'"

Even better? To pray: "Lord, I thank You for Daniel 9:2–3, which tells me that Daniel read a portion of the book of Jeremiah, took that portion's sober and hope-filled truths to heart, and then turned to You in earnest, serious, and wholehearted prayer."

In the end, all Bible study is a conversation. It's the Lord speaking to your heart, and then you responding in prayer. That's why every Bible study in this book ends with a prayer!

Pray:

Yes, Lord, I want to say "Thank You!" for today's Bible reading and key verse. Like Daniel, I want to take You at Your word and pray every day.

How to Succeed at Bible Study
Read 1 Thessalonians 3:1–13

Key Verse:

May [the Lord]. . .make your hearts strong, blameless, and holy as you stand before God our Father when our Lord Jesus comes again with all his holy people. Amen.
1 THESSALONIANS 3:13 NLT

Understand:

- *How much have you studied scripture in the past?*
- *How much do you want to study the Bible in the future?*

Apply:

In your heart, you want to be successful at Bible study. Here are five keys:

1. Make a goal. Your goal might be to finish every Bible study in this book in three months. If you miss a day, don't worry. You can squeeze in an extra 5 minutes tomorrow. Worst case? You can catch up a whole week's worth of Bible studies in 35 minutes. You can do this!

2. Divide and conquer. If your schedule doesn't allow for daily Bible study, figure out what else might work. The National Guard achieves its objectives one weekend per month through most of the year. During this particular season, what would work best for you?

3. *Study with your head and heart.* If you don't understand something, it's okay to ask questions. But as you read and study, focus on what *is* clear.

4. *Pick a favorite verse to make your own.* A good friend of mine picked 1 Thessalonians 3:13 as a prayer focus for the year. Do you have a favorite? If so, great! If not, you might discover it in this book.

5. *Talk to the Lord as you study His Word.* Literally say, "Yes, Lord, I want to live for You as Abraham and Joseph, and as Peter and Paul, did."

The master key? Taking scripture seriously. After all, it is God's Word!

Pray:

Yes, Lord, as You know, I have already said "Yes!" to reading and studying the Bible. That's why I'm spending these minutes with You again today.

The Biblical Heroes Hilkiah and Ezra

Read 2 Kings 22:1—23:3

Key Verse:

The king stood by the pillar and renewed the covenant in the presence of the LORD—to follow the LORD and keep his commands, statutes and decrees with all his heart and all his soul, thus confirming the words of the covenant written in this book. Then all the people pledged themselves to the covenant.

2 KINGS 23:3 NIV

Understand:

- *Why do you think God preserved the Hebrew scriptures?*
- *Does anyone need to wonder or worry about lost books of the Bible?*

Apply:

Again, it's common to wonder, "Do we have all the right books in God's Word?" Thankfully, the books of the Old Testament were miraculously preserved despite persecution and national apostasy.

Wicked King Manasseh reigned over Judah hundreds of years after Moses, David, and many of the other Old Testament writers. Manasseh considered nothing sacred. You could compare him to the wicked sorcerer in *Indiana Jones and the Temple of Doom*—but instead of sacrificing other people's children, he passed his own son through the fire (2 Kings 21:6)—as well as any copies of the scriptures he could find, it seems.

A generation later, not even the high priest in Jerusalem had a copy of God's Word, until the day Hilkiah the high priest exclaimed, "I have found the Book of the Law" (2 Kings 22:8). This occurred just before the Babylonian captivity of the nation of Israel in 386 BC.

Fortunately, the Israelites took the then-completed books of the Old Testament to Babylon and preserved them throughout their captivity. Hilkiah's family apparently retained the rediscovered scriptures and passed them down from generation to generation.

Hilkiah's great-grandson Ezra had a copy of the scriptures with him when he returned with the released captives to Jerusalem. He was known as a man of the Word (Ezra 7:10 and Nehemiah 8:1–3).

Pray:

Yes, Lord, I want to say "Thank You!" for preserving each and every book of the Bible. Even in the worst of times, You used Hilkiah and Ezra in remarkable ways.

How to Experience the Bible's Vistas and Rewards
Read Colossians 3:1–17

Key Verse:

Let the word of Christ dwell in you richly.
COLOSSIANS 3:16 ESV

Understand:

- *What's the biggest difference when a Christian and an atheist study the Bible?*
- *When does a Christian see the most in scripture?*

Apply:

Congratulations for doing the first seven Bible studies! Remember how you feel when you see a strikingly beautiful place for the first time? When you study the Bible, you want to do so with your spiritual eyes wide open. How do you do that?

First, you come to God in prayer. You can worship God, thank Him for His Word, and then ask Him to remove anything that would cloud your heart and mind as you read and study the Bible.

Second, you ask God for the Holy Spirit's illumination as you read each passage of scripture. You can read the same passage of scripture two, three, four, or more times and still make new discoveries with each new reading.

Third, you come to the Bible with a strong sense of expectancy, determination, and persistence. You want to look closely at scripture. The goal of such careful observation is to discover more and more of what the Word says.

You're not doing a superficial once-over, like you're taking a cursory glance around the room to find your shoes. Instead, you're looking intently at God's Word. What awe-inspiring vistas and rewards He has in store for you in the days ahead!

Pray:

Yes, Lord, I want to say "Thank You!" for the vistas and rewards of reading and studying the Bible. I can't wait to see what You have in store for me in the days ahead.

Bible Study Isn't Too Difficult
Read Deuteronomy 29:9–30:16

Key Verse:

The secret things belong to the Lord our God, but the things revealed belong to us and to our children forever, that we may follow all the words of this law.
Deuteronomy 29:29 niv

Understand:

- *Which Bible translations have you used?*
- *Which Bible translation do you find is the easiest to understand?*

Apply:

Some guys allege that reading and studying the Bible is too hard. Wow, nothing could be further from the truth!

If Moses were here, he would shake his head and ask, "Are God's blessings only for the elite?" Instead, in Deuteronomy 29:29, he says that what God has revealed in scripture belongs to everyone, including your children. Granted, the Bible doesn't record everything God knows—not by a long shot! But scripture is everything He's given mankind, it's eternal, and it's designed as a divine imperative to action. (*Do* is the operative word!)

A few paragraphs earlier, in Deuteronomy 29:9–15, Moses said that the person who knows, respects, preserves, and carefully follows God's Word will "prosper in everything [he does]." You don't need a theological degree to read, understand, and apply the Bible to your life.

A few paragraphs later, in Deuteronomy 30:11–16, Moses said God's Word is clear enough for anyone to understand and obey—and reap God's blessings in every area of life.

The reality is that the Bible is available in several wonderful, accurate, highly readable English translations. Translations are nothing new. Jesus and the apostles read and quoted from the Greek translation of the Hebrew scriptures, since Greek was the common language of their day.

More than ever, the scriptures are accessible to anyone and everyone, including you!

Pray:

Yes, Lord, I want to say "Thank You!" for designing the Bible and doing Bible study so both are accessible to guys like me. I'm motivated to keep going because I want to reap Your blessings in every area of my life. Help me recognize each of those blessings in the days and weeks ahead.

Excuses for Not Studying the Bible
Read Matthew 15:1–20

Key Verse:

Then Jesus called to the crowd to come and hear.
"Listen," he said, "and try to understand."
MATTHEW 15:10 NLT

Understand:

- *How much can personal issues color or cloud a man's understanding of God's Word?*
- *How willing are you to believe what Jesus says?*

Apply:

What are some excuses guys give for not studying the Bible?

1. "No one studies the Bible." The truth is, one in five American adults say they read and study the Bible regularly. If you don't know anyone who does, ask around. If someone you ask says they don't study the Bible, ask if they would be interested in studying it with you. Don't be surprised if several say yes! When they do, encourage them to buy this book and go through it along with you.

2. "No time to study the Bible." This is like saying

you don't have time to eat, drink, or sleep. Are you willing to take five minutes to read and study scripture daily? If so, in three months you'll finish every Bible study in this book. This is doable!

3. *"The Bible is full of errors."* Actually, this line of thinking is what's in error. The Bible is completely accurate and wholly trustworthy.

4. *"It makes me feel guilty."* Now here's an honest excuse! It's true, but it's important to note that God's purpose isn't to make you feel guilty. Instead, in Psalm 119:9–11, you read that scripture keeps you pure. In John 15:3 and 17:17, Jesus reiterated the truth that God's Word makes you holy.

Ultimately, there's no good excuse for not studying the Bible—and plenty of good reasons to study it!

Pray:

Yes, Lord, I want to say no to any and all excuses that might tempt me to stop reading and studying Your Word. Instead, I'm saying yes to You again today.

Natural and Supernatural Revelations
Read Titus 1:1–2:15

Key Verse:

Teach them to know the truth that shows them how to live godly lives. This truth gives them confidence that they have eternal life, which God—who does not lie—promised them before the world began.
TITUS 1:1–2 NLT

Understand:

- *Which kind of general revelation do you value the most?*
- *Which kind of special revelation do you value the most?*

Apply:

It's common to ask, "What else did God give us besides the Bible?" Thankfully, God has chosen to reveal Himself in many ways. *General revelations* are God's self-disclosure through *natural* means to all men. Five examples follow below:

- Creation (Romans 1:18–21). Why is there an ordered universe?
- Preservation (Colossians 1:17). Why doesn't it all fall apart?

- Providence (Acts 14:17). Why do good things happen to bad people?
- Conscience (Romans 2:15). Why do we have a sense of right and wrong?
- Reason (Acts 17:16–34). What is "obvious" about the unknown God?

Special revelations are God's self-disclosure of His message through *supernatural* means to some for all mankind. Here are five examples:

- Theophanies, or special appearances by the Lord (Genesis 18:1–2). The Lord revealed Himself in the form of men and angels.
- Visions (1 Samuel 3:1–4 and Acts 16:9). The Lord speaks in dreams and angelic appearances.
- Jesus Christ (John 1:1–18 and Hebrews 1:1–2). God spoke through His Son.
- Prophecies (1 Kings 17:1 and Titus 1:1–3). The Lord spoke to the prophets, giving oral messages to Israel and the nations.
- Inspiration (2 Timothy 3:16–17 and 2 Peter 1:20–21). The Lord directed the prophets and apostles to write certain messages.

You might envy those who received special revelations from the Lord. Yet you are more privileged than those of any other age, because you have free access to the entire Word of God.

Pray:

Yes, Lord, I want to say "Wow!" for the rewards I experience as I keep reading and studying Your Word.

Simple and Complex Truths
Read Isaiah 55:1–13

Key Verse:

*For as the heavens are higher than the earth,
so are my ways higher than your ways and
my thoughts than your thoughts.*
ISAIAH 55:9 ESV

Understand:

- *Remember phone books? A million facts,
  but none that could change your life.*
- *The Bible has more than 31,100 verses.
  How many can change your life?*

Apply:

The Bible is truer than any other book ever published. The Bible was written by God. It will *never* be out of date. Your belief in the Bible is based on the fact that God *always* tells the truth. It is a book of *trustworthy facts about eternal realities.*

As you examine how Jesus and the apostles viewed the Old Testament, you come to understand that they believed the scriptures are not only a revelation *from* God but also a revelation *of* God. They accepted the factual statements in the Bible at face value and then saw the spiritual implications of its important truths.

In the Bible, you find two kinds of facts: *simple* truths (easily grasped facts) and *complex* truths (facts that exceed your grasp). You will never plumb the depths of the Bible's complex truths. God's thoughts far exceed the collective brainpower of *all* humanity (Isaiah 55:8–9).

It's no wonder that God doesn't pretend to tell you everything (Deuteronomy 29:29). It's also ludicrous to think you can contribute one microscopic atom of truth to what God has known before the beginning of time (Romans 11:33). He is God. You are not!

In coming days, we'll look at how to enjoy and benefit even more from reading and studying scripture.

By asking questions.

By noting specific facts.

By taking God at His Word.

Pray:

Yes, Lord, I want to say "Thank You!" for who You are. You are the Lord God, Creator of heaven and earth. Your ways are infinitely higher than my ways. I trust You!

The Value of Questions
Read John 1:19–42

Key Verse:

Jesus turned and saw them following and said to them, "What are you seeking?" And they said to him, "Rabbi" (which means Teacher), "where are you staying?"
JOHN 1:38 ESV

Understand:

- *In the key verse above, who is "them"?*
- *In that same verse, what does Jesus do right before asking them a question?*

Apply:

As you read and study the Bible, you want to remember that even the smallest details (say, a person's name) often have spiritual undertones.

Here's where you get to turn into a not-so-mild-mannered reporter. Pull out your press card and get ready to ask a stream of questions worthy of the best journalist. You can ask *Who? What? When? Where? Why?* and *How?* questions repeatedly as you read and study God's Word.

You won't ask all of these questions every time you read a scripture verse. But you can ask the most pertinent questions that come to mind after reading it.

By asking lots of *Who? What? When? Where? Why?* and *How?* questions, you get a much better idea of what any given scripture passage says. You also get a good idea of what it *doesn't* say and what you're not yet sure it's saying.

The exciting news throughout scripture is that God promises to bless the man who reads His Word, looks intently at it, interprets it correctly, personalizes it, and applies it to his life. Be that man!

Pray:

Yes, Lord, I want to say "Thank You!" for asking me to engage my brain and ask lots of questions as I read the Bible. No more autopilot for me.

Look Intently, But That's Not All
Read Psalm 49:1–20

Key Verse:

*But God will ransom my soul from the power
of Sheol, for he will receive me. Selah*
PSALM 49:15 ESV

Understand:

- *In Numbers 16:31–32, what terrible
  judgment did Korah receive?*
- *What lessons did Korah's sons learn from
  their father's demise?*

Apply:

It can be tempting to think that it's fairly easy to
discern the facts in a scripture passage. That's often
the case, but not always!

Granted, Psalm 49 isn't one of the most accessible psalms. That's all the more reason to blitz every
verse with as many questions as possible, right? You
can ask 145 questions over the course of the first six
verses alone. Of those 145 questions, only 24 can be
answered by observations made within the immediate content. The other 121 questions require interpretative answers. (Thankfully, those interpretative
answers exist!)

The key thing to remember is that the goal of Bible study isn't simply to look intently at each passage of scripture. James 1:25 (NKJV) reminds us, "But he who looks into the perfect law of liberty and continues in it, and is not a forgetful hearer but a doer of the work, this one will be blessed in what he does."

Nothing replaces the importance of the Holy Spirit's illuminating your heart and mind. Jesus sent the Spirit to take up residence in every Christian for that very reason. The Holy Spirit's greatest desire is to bring God's Word alive within you so that you can wholeheartedly love the Lord, worship Him, and do what He says!

Pray:

Yes, Lord, I want to say "Thank You!" that the Bible is an incredibly cohesive whole, not a lot of miscellaneous parts. I can learn so much from it.

God Means What He Says
Read Deuteronomy 18:1–22

Key Verse:

*Moses continued, "The LORD your God will raise
up for you a prophet like me from among your
fellow Israelites. You must listen to him."*
DEUTERONOMY 18:15 NLT

Understand:

- *Based on Acts 3:22–23, who is the
  "prophet like me"?*
- *Based on Acts 7:37, who is the "prophet
  like me"?*

Apply:

Thankfully, there's no secret code or formula for
understanding the Bible. The world's best seller is
written so people listening to or reading it can grasp
what God is saying to them. True, it's possible to
misunderstand scripture—men have done that from
day one. Still, the Lord wants you to *know* what He's
saying!

The "golden rule" of biblical interpretation says
God is not trying to mess with our minds. The
same goes for Moses, David, Ezra, Malachi, Matthew, Mark, and all the other biblical writers. They

expected listeners and readers to understand the meaning of what they wrote.

True, you may not catch everything the first time through. That's why you enjoy listening again to a favorite new song, why you're eager to watch a sports replay, and why you stop to reread something that's profound.

Because God isn't trying to trick anyone, when you're reading scripture you shouldn't try to "decode" it. Unless there's a compelling reason, you should accept the facts the Bible states at face value and embrace the normal meaning of its truths.

Pray:

Yes, Lord, I want to say "Thank You!" for designing the Bible the way You did. You're not trying to mess with me. That means a lot.

What God Means to Say
Read John 8:12–36

Key Verse:

"So if the Son sets you free,
you will be free indeed."
JOHN 8:36 NIV

Understand:

- *According to John 14:6, who is the Truth?*
- *How does He make us free?*

Apply:

Like any great writer, God had specific facts and truths in mind for every verse in scripture. The important question isn't, what does this say to *me*? Instead, the question you want to ask is, what did *God* mean?

Take the famous statement by Jesus, "The truth shall make you free" (John 8:32 NKJV). You could come up with any of a dozen misinterpretations of that verse. But in the end, it doesn't matter what you want that verse to mean.

If you consider yourself an intellectual, you may want "The truth shall make you free" to mean that the more you know and learn, the better your life will be. If you consider yourself an enlightened hedonist, you may want it to mean that you're free to do whatever you want whenever you want as long as it doesn't hurt anyone else. But these popular misinterpretations are *not* what Jesus was saying!

As you read and study the Bible, you want to keep asking, *What did God mean by this statement?* If you're not sure, that's okay! Just write down your questions and then look up the answers later in a study Bible or good Bible commentary.

Studying the Bible isn't a matter of *your* interpretation. Instead, you want to embrace the church's clear understanding of scripture.

Pray:

Yes, Lord, I want to say "Thank You!" that You want me to know what You meant by every chapter, paragraph, and verse of scripture. That's what I want to know.

Scripture Itself Answers
Many Questions
Read Jonah 1:1–2:10

Key Verse:

"But I will offer sacrifices to you with songs of praise, and I will fulfill all my vows. For my salvation comes from the LORD alone."
JONAH 2:9 NLT

Understand:

- *Do you find it easy or difficult to believe today's scripture reading?*
- *What makes it easy or difficult for you?*

Apply:

If you don't have a study Bible, it's time to buy one! If you run into several tough questions, you also can ask your pastor for permission to drop by his office to look up the answers in his commentaries.

Not all Bible commentaries, however, are created equal. In fact, some of them attack the Christian faith. If you're reading a commentary that doesn't (1) worship God, (2) praise the Lord Jesus Christ, and (3) show tremendous respect for God's Word, drop it fast and look for a better one!

Even the best Bible commentators don't have all

the answers—not by a long shot. Not every state-ment in scripture is clear-cut. Some are so poetic that it's hard to tell what the verse or paragraph means. That said, often it's as you keep reading and studying scripture that you realize, *There's the answer to one of my questions!*

Do your best to discover what *God* wants you to know. Most of the answers are right there in His Word. In the end, however, it's okay to list your unanswered questions. In some cases, you'll have to wait until heaven to ask Moses, David, Daniel, or Paul, "What did you mean by this?" or "What did you mean by that?" Imagine how great that will be!

Pray:

Yes, Lord, I want to say "Thank You!" that I can own several Bibles, including one with detailed study notes to help me more readily understand and apply Your Word. And "Thank You!" for motivating me to use this book toward that end.

Occasional Second Layer of Meaning

Read Psalm 22:1–18

Key Verse:

*They divide my garments among themselves
and throw dice for my clothing.*
PSALM 22:18 NLT

Understand:

- *Which verses in today's Bible reading remind you of the day Jesus was crucified?*
- *Which verses probably apply only to David's desperate circumstances?*

Apply:

Like any great writer, God occasionally added an important second layer of meaning to a particular word, phrase, sentence, or longer section of scripture. But that second layer of meaning always builds on—and never contradicts—the primary meaning.

In the Old Testament, you see a secondary layer of meaning most often in passages that look forward to the coming of the Messiah, Jesus Christ. Thankfully, Jesus Himself pointed out many of these passages to His disciples after His resurrection (Luke 24:26–27). The apostles studied the Hebrew scriptures diligently after Jesus's ascension (Acts 1:15–22). The apostle Paul did the same thing after his conversion (Acts 9:20–22).

If you think there might be a secondary meaning to a specific Old Testament verse, that's great! Write down your question and then look up the answer in your study Bible or a good commentary.

Just be careful not to spend too much time focused on or worried about possible secondary layers of meaning as you read the Bible. Unless something jumps out at you, keep your focus on the main thing God meant to say.

Pray:

Yes, Lord, I want to say "Thank You!" for the many
ways the Old Testament scriptures point to
Your Son and my Lord and Savior,
Jesus Christ. He's the real hero!

Figures of Speech Have Known Meaning

Read John 15:1–17

Key Verse:

*"I am the true grapevine,
and my Father is the gardener."*
JOHN 15:1 NLT

Understand:

- *In the Old Testament's first five books, God promised to reward His people for doing something. The blessings include fruitful vineyards. What do you think He wanted them to do?*
- *In the Old Testament's second half, God compared His people to vineyards ready to be utterly destroyed. What do you think they did to deserve such severe judgment?*

Apply:

Like any great writer, God used hyperbole, simile, metaphor, and other figures of speech throughout the Old and New Testaments. Not surprisingly, during His time on earth, the Lord Jesus often used figures of speech whenever He spoke to the crowds.

True, figures of speech sometimes confuse listeners and readers. But they're memorable and often cause readers to stop and wonder, *What did Jesus mean by that?* Thankfully, His figures of speech almost always have a known meaning.

If you run across a figure of speech in the Bible that you haven't heard before, try looking it up in your favorite online English language dictionary. Many English figures of speech have biblical roots. If that doesn't work, look it up in your study Bible.

Five famous figures of speech in the Gospel of Matthew follow below:

- "Follow Me, and I will make you fishers of men" (4:19).
- "You are the salt of the earth" (5:13).
- "For John came neither eating nor drinking" (11:18).
- "It is easier for a camel to go through the eye of a needle than for a rich man to enter the kingdom of God" (19:24).
- "Woe to you, scribes and Pharisees, hypocrites! For you are like whitewashed tombs" (23:27).

Pray:

Yes, Lord, I want to say "Thank You!" for the creativity built into the design of language. It makes Your Word all the more interesting, provocative, and life-changing.

The Bible's Rich Vocabulary
Read 1 Samuel 15:10–35

Key Verse:

*The LORD regretted that He had
made Saul king over Israel.*
1 SAMUEL 15:35 NKJV

Understand:

- *You "hope" the weather is better
  tomorrow. How is that different from
  "hope" in the New Testament?*
- *Looking back on your life, you likely have
  "regrets." How is that different from the
  Bible saying God "regretted" something?*

Apply:

Like any great writer, God used a rich vocabulary. So,
not surprisingly, God's Word will stretch even the
most avid reader's vocabulary.

It's important to remember that the biblical
author determines the meaning of a given word.
What does the Bible mean when it says God "regretted"? Of course, there's more than one meaning for
that word. A good dictionary may list five possible
definitions. Then again, the Bible may add a sixth
meaning.

The good news is you can use a standard collegiate dictionary to look up the meaning of most words you'll find in the Bible. Still, you may run into a few words that you'll find only in a twenty-five-pound unabridged dictionary.

If that's the case, see if your study Bible tells you what it means. Also, read the same verse in one or two other contemporary Bible translations. You may even want to look up the word on BibleGateway .com. It can give you a list of other verses—in one or more Bible translations—that use that same word.

Pray:

Yes, Lord, I want to say "Thank You!" for Your infinite wisdom and way with words. Thank You for the many resources we have to better understand Your Word.

New Uses for Old Words
Read Ephesians 3:1–11

Key Verse:

This mystery is that through the gospel the Gentiles are heirs together with Israel, members together of one body, and sharers together in the promise in Christ Jesus.
Ephesians 3:6 niv

Understand:

- *What do you think Charles Dickens meant when he quipped, "The life of Shakespeare is a fine mystery"?*
- *What do you think the apostle Paul meant when he used the word mystery?*

Apply:

Like William Shakespeare, Mark Twain, and Ernest Hemingway, God sometimes chose to use an old word in a new way. You see this in Paul's New Testament letters.

Paul used the word *mystery* often. That word already had several definitions. If you look up all of Paul's uses of the word, you'll discover that it referred to the new revelations God had given the apostles through Jesus Christ and the Holy Spirit.

One of those new revelations is the "mystery"

that God designed the church to be composed of *all* people—Jewish and Gentile (anyone who's not Jewish), male and female, slave and free.

In other words, God wants everyone to turn from his sins, turn to God, trust Jesus Christ, and instantly become a member of the church, which includes everyone who is a real Christian. You may take that for granted today, but it was a brand-new idea 2,000 years ago!

Pray:

Yes, Lord, I want to say "Thank You!" for the many ways the New Testament reveals the transforming power of the Gospel of Jesus Christ. That Good News has changed my life here and now, and for eternity.

Occasional Power-Packed Words
Read Galatians 3:1–14

Key Verse:

And the Scripture, foreseeing that God would justify the Gentiles by faith, preached the gospel beforehand to Abraham, saying, "In you shall all the nations be blessed."
GALATIANS 3:8 ESV

Understand:

- *Sometimes a single English word, such as fellowship, takes a sentence or two to define. Why is that?*
- *Sometimes a biblical word, such as gospel, takes two or three sentences to define. Why is that?*

Apply:

Sometimes biblical writers chose to cut and paste parts of old words to create a new word. Not surprisingly, you see this in the Old Testament and in Paul's letters.

In Galatians 3:8, Paul used a word that in Greek combines the words "before" and "gospel." You don't find this compound word anywhere else in the Bible. That doesn't mean the early church didn't talk about it!

If you look it up in your Bible, you'll discover this compound term means "preached the Gospel beforehand." To communicate that concept succinctly, Paul used what may have been a new word to many of his readers. It was his shorthand way of saying a lot in one power-packed term.

If you look really hard, you'll find only a small handful of biblical words where translators have had to add a footnote saying, in effect, "We don't know for sure what this word means." Many of these words are Hebrew musical terms.

Only one undefined word appears frequently in the Bible, and then almost exclusively in one book. It's the word *selah*, which appears in the text of thirty-nine psalms. Translators have offered several possible meanings for *selah*. Whenever you run into the word, assume it means, "Think about what God is saying in this psalm. Pay attention. Now, keep reading!"

Pray:

Yes, Lord, I want to say "Thank You!" that we can understand 99.99 percent of the Bible's words and sentences in any contemporary English translation. That's amazing.

What Does the Bible Mean?
Read Genesis 4:1–16

Key Verse:

Now Cain talked with Abel his brother; and it came to pass, when they were in the field, that Cain rose up against Abel his brother and killed him.
GENESIS 4:8 NKJV

Understand:

- *The New King James Version translators added the title "Cain Murders Abel" above today's scripture reading. Why do you suppose they used the word killed in today's key verse?*
- *Why do you suppose dozens of English Bible translations haven't used the word murdered in today's key verse?*

Apply:

Like any great writer, God wrote every word and verse in context. He didn't write in a random, arbitrary manner. God has clearly communicated the meaning of most words and virtually all sentences and paragraphs within the same chapter, book, or section of the Bible. In many cases, you can figure out what God meant if you keep reading.

When you can't figure out the meaning of a statement in its immediate context, you may want to look at the broader context. In the Ten Commandments, God declared, "You shall not murder" (Exodus 20:13 and Deuteronomy 5:17). Does this verse mean "Don't kill any life form"? No. The broader context is clear. Does it mean "God is against all killing, including war and capital punishment"? No. This commandment says it's against God's law for an individual to maliciously kill another human being. The broader context even goes on to say what to do if someone accidentally kills another human being.

In the Gospels, Jesus declared, "I am the bread of life" (John 6:35). Without even studying the context, you know Jesus was using a figure of speech. Every figure of speech has a known meaning. You can determine that meaning by reading what Jesus said in context. The immediate context tells you that Jesus was saying, in effect, "I have come from God to offer you new, eternal life. You can receive that life by believing Me!"

Pray:

Yes, Lord, I want to say "Thank You!" that the Bible itself answers most of the questions I might ask. That's why I want to keep reading and studying it. The more questions I raise, the better.

Joseph and God-Inspired Dreams
Read Genesis 37:1–26

Key Verse:

*Soon Joseph had another dream, and again he
told his brothers about it. "Listen, I have had
another dream," he said. "The sun, moon,
and eleven stars bowed low before me!"*
GENESIS 37:9 NLT

Understand:

- *When it comes to new novels and movies,
  are you for or against spoiler alerts?*
- *Do you remember reading Genesis 37–50
  for the first time? If so, what surprised
  you the most?*

Apply:

Like Shakespeare, Twain, and Hemingway, God
sometimes says something you don't understand
until later in the book. In Genesis 37, you meet
Joseph as a seventeen-year-old and are immediately
told about two God-inspired dreams. Both have a
single interpretation that inflames the hatred of
his brothers, who sell Joseph into slavery in Egypt.
Joseph's dreams are utterly destroyed. Worse, after
being falsely accused of a terrible crime, Joseph

spends years in prison.

More than a decade later, two of Joseph's fellow prisoners tell him about their dreams. The dreams sound similar, but Joseph interprets them in two very different ways. Two years later, Joseph is called before Pharaoh to interpret two very disturbing dreams.

This dream motif continues until you get to the climax of Joseph's story in Genesis 45. Finally, trembling and bowing before Pharaoh's right-hand man in Egypt, absolutely afraid for their lives, Joseph's brothers receive the shock of their lives. Joseph's teenage dreams had come true before their very eyes!

Like any great book, the Bible is meant to be read over and over. Better yet, think of it like watching one of your all-time favorite movies. Remember all the "aha!" moments you had the second time you watched the movie? If you keep looking at the context, you can also have "aha!" moments every time you read and study a particular scripture passage.

Pray:

Yes, Lord, I want to say "Thank You!" for the dynamic storytelling power of many big blocks of scripture in both the Old Testament and the New Testament.

God Wanted the Bible to Have Repetition
Read Hebrews 1:1–2:4

Key Verse:

Long ago, at many times and in many ways,
God spoke to our fathers by the prophets.
HEBREWS 1:1 ESV

Understand:

- *An old Latin proverb says, "Repetition is the mother of learning." Why do you think that is?*
- *When you read the Gospels, what do you think about parallel accounts of Jesus' teachings and miracles?*

Apply:

Like any great writer, God wrote more than one work. Since the Bible is a collection of sixty-six God-inspired books with a unified theme and purpose, it's well worth your time comparing one scripture passage with other related passages.

Many study Bibles provide a list of cross-references for any given scripture verse. The cross-references show how other verses address the same theme. In addition, most study Bibles let you know whenever there's a parallel passage to the one you're reading. For example:

- You'll find that Moses covers many of the events and laws in Exodus, Leviticus, and Numbers all over again in Deuteronomy.
- You'll find many of the events in 1 and 2 Samuel and 1 and 2 Kings covered again from a different perspective in 1 and 2 Chronicles.
- You'll find many direct and indirect Old Testament quotations throughout the New Testament. Many show how Jesus is the promised Messiah.
- You'll find a number of Jesus' miracles and teachings covered from different perspectives in two or three Gospels.
- You'll find a number of the apostles' teachings and instructions covered from different perspectives in multiple New Testament letters.

The good news is that the more time you spend seeking to understand scripture correctly, the easier it gets. God designed it that way!

Pray:

Yes, Lord, I want to say "Thank You!" for letting me know the important themes in scripture by repeating them and expressing them in so many different ways.

How Big Is God?
Read Genesis 1:1–31

Key Verse:

*And God blessed them. And God said to them,
"Be fruitful and multiply and fill the earth and subdue
it, and have dominion over the fish of the sea and
over the birds of the heavens and over every
living thing that moves on the earth."*
GENESIS 1:28 ESV

Understand:

- *What does the first chapter of the Bible
  tell us about God?*
- *What does it tell us about mankind?*

Apply:

God's Word is relevant to all men, everywhere, every time. According to 2 Timothy 3:16–17, all scripture is inspired by God and is useful, profitable, beneficial, practical, and full of rewards for the person who studies it.

The Bible contains truths, commands, and examples that speak directly to your heart and life today. It's full of countless amazing truths about God, your life, and things to come.

Sometimes the trick, however, is determining

how to study the Bible when you're in a particular situation. The problem? You're often in a hurry to know which way to turn! How much better to slow down and check your God-given map for life. Even better, why not plot your course ahead of time? After all, the road ahead isn't about to move!

You can't find ten words more powerful than the Bible's opening line: "In the beginning God created the heavens and the earth" (Genesis 1:1). Talk about *great!* On the sixth day, He made man (Genesis 1:26–27). Yet miracles are only ripples of God's first words. He isn't finished speaking yet!

No matter what challenges you face between here and heaven, God is big enough to meet your needs. He'll never say, "Whoa! Now *that's* a problem. You're on your own this time."

Pray:

Yes, Lord, I want to say "Thank You!" again that You could but speak the word and create the entire universe. Yet You know and care about us. You love me. I'm humbled and amazed.

God Is Great, Good, and Gracious
Read Ephesians 1:1–14

Key Verse:

He predestined us for adoption to sonship through Jesus Christ, in accordance with his pleasure and will.
EPHESIANS 1:5 NIV

Understand:

- *According to today's key verse, how long has God planned on adopting you?*
- *According to the same verse, why did God plan to do this?*

Apply:

It's good to remember that no matter what challenges you face, God in His infinite and eternal greatness is plenty big enough to meet your needs. Again, He'll never say, "Whoa, now *that's* a problem. You're on your own this time."

God is great *and* good. Forget about a second honeymoon on a remote South Pacific isle. You can't ask for anything better than the Garden of Eden (Genesis 2:8–25). Adam and Eve had it made. Yet Paradise is only God's first act. He's saving His best for last! From now until eternity, God will always do what is truly best for us. He'll never be tempted to say, "I'm tired of all this righteous stuff. I feel like changing all the rules today. Watch out, world!"

What's more, God is gracious. Forget getting out of jail free. You can't thank God enough for showing mercy and promising a Redeemer. The wages of man's sin was death (Romans 6:23). Yet forgiveness is only God's first gift. He's promised you so much more!

You can always count on the fact that God has much more than salvation in store for us. He will always be glad to say, "Can I tell you again how much I love you? I'm so glad you're My child."

Pray:

Yes, Lord, I want to say "Thank You!"
for Your incredible love for me.
It's astounding. I love You too.

Peace with God, Others, and Your Circumstances
Read Philippians 4:1–23

Key Verse:

Finally, brothers, whatever is true, whatever is honorable, whatever is just, whatever is pure, whatever is lovely, whatever is commendable, if there is any excellence, if there is anything worthy of praise, think about these things.
PHILIPPIANS 4:8 ESV

Understand:

- *Where was the apostle Paul when he wrote his letter to the Philippian church?*
- *How often do you think Paul had practiced what he preached?*

Apply:

Surprisingly, the simplest questions are sometimes the most profound. This is especially true when you're considering what God has to say to you in His Word. Sadly, many Christian men feel personalizing scripture has to be complicated. Nothing is further from the truth!

Here are six simple yet profound questions. They can quickly transform ordinary Bible study into a life-changing experience. As you read a phrase, verse, or short paragraph of scripture, ask yourself these three sets of questions.

- What Truths does this passage teach? Do you Affirm them?
- What Commands does the Lord give? Do you Obey them?
- What Examples does this scripture present? Do you Heed them?

This is the **TA-CO, EH?** (Truths to Affirm, Commands to Obey, Examples to Heed) approach to personalized scripture reading. It works great no matter where you live (Mexico or Canada, in between, or overseas), how you prefer to talk (*si*, eh, or yes), or what you like to eat!

TA-CO, EH? is the secret sauce of Bible study for men. Think of this as a bottle of your favorite hot pepper mixture. Over the next few days, get ready for spicier Bible studies!

Pray:

Yes, Lord, I want to say "Thank You!" for the memorable TA-CO, EH? acronym. Even better, thanks that three simple sets of questions quickly and readily show me how to apply Your Word to my life today.

John 3:16 Truths to Affirm
Read John 3:1–16

Key Verse:

"For God so loved the world that He gave His only begotten Son, that whoever believes in Him should not perish but have everlasting life."
JOHN 3:16 NKJV

Understand:

- *Imagine you could share one Bible verse with everyone you know. Why would John 3:16 be a good choice?*
- *What other single Bible verse would you share with everyone you know?*

Apply:

Let's begin by asking: what Truths to Affirm does today's famous key verse teach? Looking at the verse itself, you discover some important truths:

- God loves the world.
- God loves you so much He sent His only Son.
- Whoever believes in Him will not perish.
- Whoever believes in Him will have everlasting life.

These basic truths, however, don't tell you

everything you want to know. If it's so important to believe in God's only Son, who is He? Where was He sent? And why? Thankfully, you can look at this same verse from an informed New Testament perspective, and then readily affirm four more truths:

- God loves the world (everyone, including you).
- God loves you so much He sent His only Son (Jesus Christ, who died on a Roman cross in your place for your sins).
- Whoever believes in Him (Jesus Christ) will not perish (remain spiritually dead here on earth and afterward go to hell).
- Whoever believes in Him (Jesus Christ) will have everlasting life (enjoy spiritual life here on earth and afterward go to heaven).

No wonder John 3:16 is the most loved verse in all scripture!

Caveat: Not all truths are created equal. Scripture accurately records outright lies, straightforward historical details, insights about how life works, and divinely revealed truths. The Bible itself places the most value on the latter.

Pray:

Yes, Lord, I want to say "Thank You!" for these rich and life-changing truths. No wonder John 3:16 is such a famous and memorable verse.

John 3:16 Commands to Obey
Read John 3:16–21

Key Verse:

"For God so loved the world that he gave his one and only Son, that whoever believes in him shall not perish but have eternal life."
JOHN 3:16 NIV

Understand:

- *What verbs do you see in today's key verse?*
- *Who loved and gave? And, who believes?*

Apply:

Now it's time to ask: what Commands to Obey does the Lord give in today's key verse?

The verse itself doesn't contain any commands, but it implies the most important command the Lord gives in all scripture. This is a command you find throughout the New Testament, and it is especially prevalent in John's writings. The implied command is this: *believe in Jesus Christ.*

Again, John 3:16 doesn't state a direct command: "The Lord says to everyone, everywhere, for all of time, 'Believe in My only Son, Jesus Christ.'" But that imperative is embedded at the core of the verse in the phrase "believes in Him."

Whenever you see a powerful verb in scripture, you want to ask yourself, *Does this verb imply a biblical command? If so, what is that command?*

If you're reading the Bible for the very first time, and you've read only snatches here and there, you may not be able to *see* the implied commands of scripture. With time, however, you'll see them on every page!

Caveat: Not all commands are created equal. Some commands are perpetual, other commands have clearly expired, and still others are for someone else—not for you.

Pray:

Yes, Lord, I want to say "Thank You!" for moving my heart months or years ago to believe in Your Son and my Lord and Savior, Jesus Christ. I still believe!

John 3:16 Examples to Heed
Read John 3:16–36

Key Verse:

"For this is how God loved the world: He gave his one and only Son, so that everyone who believes in him will not perish but have eternal life."
JOHN 3:16 NLT

Understand:

- *What are the best things about following God's examples?*
- *What are some of the hardest things about following God's examples?*

Apply:

Last but not least, it's time to ask: what Examples to Heed does this verse present?

In this single verse, you find two important examples:

- God loves the world.
- God sent His only Son.

What do these examples show us? The rest of John's gospel communicates two more important truths:

- Just as God loves the world, so you

should love all people, whether or not they believe in Jesus Christ.

- Just as God sent His only Son, so you should give sacrificially so others can accept God's love, believe in Jesus Christ, and receive eternal life.

After Jesus Christ's resurrection and ascension to heaven, the apostle John himself embraced both of these examples and faithfully lived them out for the rest of his life. They're worthy examples to imitate today and for the rest of your life.

Caveat: Not all examples are created equal. Some examples are positive, some are negative, and some don't apply to you.

Pray:

Yes, Lord, I want to say "Thank You!" for Your incredible demonstrations of sacrificial love. In turn, I want to love You more. May I discover the secret of loving You with all my heart, soul, strength, and mind.

What to Do in a Crisis
Read Psalm 3:1–8

Key Verse:

LORD, how many are my foes!
How many rise up against me!
PSALM 3:1 NIV

Understand:

- *Do you think your emotions ever shock or surprise God?*
- *Or do you feel free to tell God exactly how you feel?*

Apply:

With practice, you can learn how to apply the TA-CO, EH? questions to longer paragraphs and chapters of the Bible.

This works even for whole books of the Bible. Take the book of Psalms, for instance. One of the overarching *examples* you see in Psalms is how to turn to God and pray in the midst of crisis.

Beginning with Psalm 3, and over and over again until Psalm 149, you find the psalmist crying out to the Lord in various dire circumstances:

- Give me relief from my distress.

- Listen to my cry for help.
- Away from me, all you who do evil.
- Save and deliver me from all who pursue me.

In seven out of every ten psalms, the writer either cries out to the Lord for physical salvation, thanks God for sparing his life, reminds himself of the differing fates of the righteous and evildoers, or renews his allegiance to God and His Word in the face of rampant wickedness.

If Psalms teaches you anything, then it's *how* to turn to God in times of trouble and distress.

You may not be facing a crisis today—but crises will come. When they do, turn to Psalms to find comfort, solace, encouragement, joy, and strength to face each day.

Pray:

Yes, Lord, I want to say "Thank You!" that You are right here with me when life is good and when life is bad. Right now, it's a bit of both. Today, please increase my trust in You.

Time to Take Action!
Read James 2:1–26

Key Verse:

*You say you have faith, for you believe that there
is one God. Good for you! Even the demons
believe this, and they tremble in terror.*
JAMES 2:19 NLT

Understand:

- *Why isn't mental assent of biblical facts
  good enough?*
- *Why is intentional obedience to God's
  Word so important?*

Apply:

Remarkably, you can read page after page of the
Bible without ever stopping to ask, *Do I really believe
this? And this? And that?* Yet if you don't wholeheartedly affirm the Bible's truths, you can easily lose your
way in this crazy, confusing, mixed-up world of half-
truths, misconceptions, and outright lies.

It's important to read and study God's Word,
make no mistake. But it's even more important for
you to actively say yes to scripture's rich and trustworthy declarations about God, creation, the Fall,
the ancient world, God's chosen people, and God's

love for the whole world; about Jesus's life, ministry, teaching, miracles, betrayal, death, burial, and resurrection; and about the church's miraculous birth, expansion, teachings, and blessed hope.

Without affirmation and application, scripture makes no more difference in your life than water in a cooler, coffee behind the counter, or an energy drink commercial on TV. Nothing happens without deliberate *action*.

As we've discussed, three simple question sets can quickly transform ordinary Bible study into a profound, life-changing experience.

- What Truths does this passage teach? Do you Affirm them?
- What Commands does the Lord give? Do you Obey them?
- What Examples does this scripture present? Do you Heed them?

This TA-CO, EH? approach not only invigorates your experience each time you study a passage of scripture, but it can also change your life!

Pray:

Yes, Lord, I want to say "Thank You!" that You have infused scripture with Your wisdom and power and love. May I experience You on every page I read.

Don't Give Up, Quit, or Walk Away
Read 2 Timothy 4:1–18

Key Verse:

*The Lord will rescue me from every evil attack and
will bring me safely to his heavenly kingdom.
To him be glory for ever and ever. Amen.*
2 TIMOTHY 4:18 NIV

Understand:

- *In verse 5 of today's scripture reading,
  what does Paul encourage Timothy to do?*
- *In verse 7, what does Paul declare about
  his own life and ministry?*

Apply:

How important is all this? Here is one man's story:

During a profound time of crisis, I suddenly
stopped reading and studying the Bible, after reading
it daily since I was a young teenager. I couldn't even
pray. After several shattering back-to-back trials, I
had wrongly concluded that God's own hand was
crushing me.

Days went by. Weeks. Finally, in desperation, I
opened my Bible again. I knew I couldn't immediately read page after page, as had been my custom.
So I simply read one verse, and then asked myself,

Do you believe this?

Thankfully, my answer was yes. Not a *huge* yes, but a yes nevertheless. That gave me the courage to read another verse. And another. In time, God restored my faith in a remarkable way. I'll never be the same.

Today, I delight in opening God's Word and affirming what He says. And when crises come—and they always will—I'm more confident than ever that the Lord hasn't changed. He's still great. He's still good. And He's still graciously at work in my heart and life. I can't thank Him enough!

Pray:

Yes, Lord, I want to say "Thank You!" that the Bible is true to life. What an example Paul set for us. Like him, I want to finish well.

Examples of Truths to Affirm
Read 1 John 1:1–10

Key Verse:

*If we claim to be without sin, we deceive
ourselves and the truth is not in us.*
1 JOHN 1:8 NIV

Understand:

- *What does today's key verse say about
  affirming or denying what's true?*
- *Why is affirming biblical truths
  important in your everyday life?*

Apply:

It isn't enough to mentally assent to the truths of
scripture. To apply them to your life, you want to
actively and wholeheartedly *affirm* them!

How does Truths to Affirm actually work? Let's
consider a few examples from the opening pages of
Genesis and 1 John.

In Genesis 1:27, God's Word says, "So God
created mankind in his own image, in the image of
God he created them; male and female he created
them" (NIV). In response to this verse, you can readily
affirm, "I believe every person is created in the image
of God." You also can affirm, "I believe *I* am created

in the image of God." The key is to silently ask, *Do I really believe this?* If you do, you begin to gain a clearer picture of God and of yourself.

First John 1:9 (NIV) says, "If we confess our sins, he [God] is faithful and just and will forgive us our sins and purify us from all unrighteousness." In response, you can affirm, "I believe God truly forgives me when I confess my sins." The key is to affirm this in prayer to the Lord Himself, and to honestly tell Him if you have any struggles or doubts.

Pray:

Yes, Lord, I want to say "Thank You!" for forgiving all of my sins, past, present, and future. Please forgive me for what I've done wrong over the past day.

Samples of Commands to Obey
Read 2 Peter 3:1–18

Key Verse:

But according to his promise we are waiting for new heavens and a new earth in which righteousness dwells.
2 PETER 3:13 ESV

Understand:

- *Do you know anyone who says he isn't a Christian anymore? If so, what reasons does he give?*
- *Which is easier: to believe the truths of scripture or obey its New Testament commands?*

Apply:

It isn't enough to *notice* the commands in the Bible. To apply them to your life, you want to gladly and consistently *obey* them.

How does Commands to Obey actually work? Let's consider a few examples from Exodus and 2 Peter.

In Exodus 20:12 (ESV; also in Leviticus 19:3, Deuteronomy 5:16, Matthew 15:4, Mark 7:10, Luke 18:20, and Ephesians 6:2) the Lord commands us, "Honor your father and your mother." The question isn't what you think of your parents. The question is, can you honestly say, "I honor my parents in obedience to the Lord's command"? Sometimes the answer is no. If that's the case, the point isn't to heap guilt upon yourself. God simply asks you to be honest with Him and invites you to claim His promises for wisdom and strength.

In 2 Peter 3:14 you're told, "And so, dear friends, while you are waiting for these things [the new heavens and new earth] to happen, make every effort to be found living peaceful lives that are pure and blameless in [God's] sight" (NLT). Your response shouldn't be to read past this verse and pretend you're already perfect. Instead, you should decide to conform your life to scripture so you can honestly say, "I am now making every effort to live a pure and blameless life and to be at peace with God." To do that, you first want to come clean with God, and then start obeying this particular command.

Pray:

Yes, Lord, I want to say "Thank You!" for compelling us to finish well, just like Peter and Paul and other heroes of the faith. You made it clear that they weren't perfect. Yet they made every effort to keep close to You. I want to do that too.

Illustrations of Examples to Heed
Read 1 Peter 2:1–25

Key Verse:

*For God is pleased when, conscious of his will,
you patiently endure unjust treatment.*
1 PETER 2:19 NLT

Understand:

- *In Matthew 20:25–28 and John 13:13–16, Jesus instructed His disciples to follow specific examples of His. Was it easy or difficult for them to do so?*
- *The apostles Peter (1 Peter 2:18–20), Paul (Ephesians 5:1–2 and Colossians 3:13), and John (1 John 2:6 and 3:15–16) instruct believers to follow other examples of Jesus. Which one is the hardest for you?*

Apply:

It isn't enough to ponder the examples in scripture. To apply them to your life, you want to willingly and readily *heed* them.

How does Examples to Heed actually work? Let's consider a couple of examples from Leviticus and 1 Peter.

In Leviticus 8:4 you read, "So Moses followed the LORD's instructions, and the whole community assembled at the Tabernacle entrance" (NLT). You can keep reading, or you can stop, note Moses's positive example, and then affirm, "I too choose to do what the Lord commands."

In 1 Peter 2:21 (NLT), the apostle Peter spelled out the example to heed when he wrote, "For God called you to do good, even if it means suffering, just as Christ suffered for you. He is your example, and you must follow in his steps." He was calling for an immediate response. Will you say, "I follow Jesus Christ's example and am willing to suffer for doing right"?

In Joshua 1, Psalm 1, Psalm 119, 2 Peter 1, and other scriptures, God promises that He will prosper those who delight in His Word, take it to heart, and apply its truths.

Imagine what God could do in and through you if you read and studied the Bible and responded as God desired. Wow!

Pray:

Yes, Lord, I want to say "Thank You!" for the many, many examples in scripture of what to do and what not to do. I want to heed each one.

Don't Sell Yourself Short

Read Titus 2:1–15

Key Verse:

Say "No" to ungodliness and worldly passions, and to live self-controlled, upright and godly lives in this present age, while [you] wait for the blessed hope— the appearing of the glory of our great God and Savior, Jesus Christ.

Titus 2:12–13 NIV

Understand:

- *Is it enough to know what not to do? Why or why not?*
- *Is past experience helpful? Again, why or why not?*

Apply:

Never forget: you can do a 5-minute Bible study, nod your head throughout the scripture reading, and then jump out of your truck and never once stop to wonder, *What would Jesus have me do in this situation?*

Yet if you don't wholeheartedly obey the Lord's commands, you'll quickly go astray, risk your life in mad pursuit of the tempting and trivial, get terribly hurt in the process, and then have the audacity to point the finger at others—even God.

It's not enough to know the great Sunday school stories about Noah and Sarah, Joshua and Deborah, Ruth and Absalom, Elijah and Esther, Daniel and Mary, Nicodemus and Cornelius, John Mark and Timothy. True, the biblical narratives are intriguing. But what lessons can you learn from each character's faith and failings, victories and vices?

Experience truly is the best teacher—especially the experiences of others who have gone before us. So every time you study God's Word, you should seek to import lessons from the lives of both biblical scoundrels (1 Corinthians 10:1–13) and heroes of the faith (Hebrews 11:4–40).

Why hold back?

Pray:

Yes, Lord, I want to say "Thank You!" that I don't have to mess up my life. You call me to take the high road. It's steep. It's lonely sometimes. But the incredible vistas and rewards up ahead keep me going.

Scripture Speaks to Your Life
Read Romans 12:1–21

Key Verse:

*If possible, so far as it depends on you,
live peaceably with all.*
ROMANS 12:18 ESV

Understand:

- *When asked who you are, what's your best answer?*
- *Your life usually encompasses how many different areas?*

Apply:

Scripture speaks to every fiber of your being. It speaks to your looks and health, to your attitudes and actions, to your relationships with family and friends, to your use of time and money, to your employment and career options, to your educational and athletic pursuits, to your beliefs and convictions about God and the Bible.

Scripture also speaks to your interests in literature and movies, to your love of sports and music, to your hobbies and habits, to your Christian commitment and love for the Lord.

In other words, scripture speaks to *all of life*!

That's why it's crucial to read and study God's Word with a clear sense of *who you are.* How well do you understand your strengths and weaknesses, your current situation, your relationships with others, your relationship with God? Actively bring that understanding to the table when you study the Bible.

That's why it's also so important to *meditate on scripture.* It's not enough just to read the words on the page. You want to wash your mind with God's Word. Meditation involves any of these three actions:

- Reflecting on the meaning of key words in a Bible phrase, verse, or paragraph
- Memorizing a verse, paragraph, or longer section of God's Word
- Rewriting a scripture passage in your own words

Pray:

Yes, Lord, I want to say "Thank You!" for today's key verse. It's such a great reminder that You know exactly what life is like here on earth. If I could ask for one miracle, I pray that I can be reconciled and at peace with one particular person.

Seeing the Bigger Picture
Read Luke 2:1–20

Key Verse:

Joseph also went up from Galilee, out of the city of Nazareth, into Judea, to the city of David, which is called Bethlehem, because he was of the house and lineage of David.
LUKE 2:4 NKJV

Understand:

- *In* A Charlie Brown Christmas, *Linus famously quotes Luke 2:8–14. After the angels disappeared, what did the shepherds do?*
- *For the rest of their lives, what did the shepherds know was true?*

Apply:

The average man has nearly a dozen areas of life. Some areas overlap with others. Many don't. Remarkably, scripture speaks to every area.

Using the TA-CO, EH? questions, you can find thousands of relevant truths, commands, and examples from Genesis through Revelation.

Because scripture speaks to all of life, you also want to prayerfully talk with God about what He says about each area. In many ways, prayer is the most important tool for Bible study. One great prayer: "Lord, please help me see Your bigger picture as I read Your Word."

When the Old Testament prophets predicted the coming of the Messiah, Jesus Christ, they couldn't see the bigger picture. Collectively, they said the Messiah would come from at least six different places.

1. Bethlehem (Micah 5:2)
2. Egypt (Hosea 11:1)
3. Galilee (Isaiah 9:1)
4. Jerusalem (Zechariah 9:9)
5. The Mount of Olives (Zechariah 14:4)
6. The temple (Malachi 3:1)

Who was right? They all were. It isn't until you pray, read, and study the four Gospels, however, that you can put this all together.

Pray:

Yes, Lord, I want to say "Thank You!" that You want to keep bringing me up to new vistas where I can see the bigger pictures in Your Word.

God Promises Great Blessings!

Read Psalm 1:1–6

Key Verse:

But his delight is in the law of the Lord,
and on his law he meditates day and night.
PSALM 1:2 ESV

Understand:

- *Does it surprise you that God promises*
  incredible blessings? Why or why not?
- *Does it seem hard to believe that God*
  promises such blessings? Why or why not?

Apply:

Scripture itself teaches that God prospers those who delight in His Word, take it to heart, and apply it in every area of life. How do we know that? Here are four reasons:

1. In Joshua 1:7–9, God promises "you will make your way prosperous" (successful in each area of life) if you study His Word, meditate on it daily, and faithfully obey His commands. What more could we ask?

2. In Psalm 1:1–3, God promises that anyone who delights in obeying His Word and meditates on it daily will prosper in "whatever he does." Why

would He repeat such an extravagant promise? Because God wants us to take Him at His Word!

3. In Psalm 19:7–14, David said God's Word revives our souls, makes us wise, brings us joy, and gives us insight into life if we desire it, delight in it, listen to it, obey it, confess any known sins, and seek to please the Lord.

4. In Psalm 119:97–104, the psalmist said he loved God's Word, which made him wiser than his enemies, his teachers, and his elders, for he desired scripture, meditated on it "all the day," and always obeyed it.

That's not all that God promises. There's more!

Pray:

Yes, Lord, I want to say "Thank You!" for encouraging me to read and study the Bible—and for promising so many blessings if I take You at Your Word.

God Promises More Great Blessings!
Read James 1:1–27

Key Verse:

But if you look carefully into the perfect law that sets you free, and if you do what it says and don't forget what you heard, then God will bless you for doing it.
JAMES 1:25 NLT

Understand:

- *Do you ever worry that God's promises might be too good to be true?*
- *Then again, do you ever worry about God blessing you too much?*

Apply:

Again, God prospers those who delight in His Word, take it to heart, and apply it in every area of life. How do we know that? Here are four more reasons:

5. In Jeremiah 15:16–17 and Ezekiel 3:1–11, the prophets described God's Word as sweet as honey, despite the difficult mission God gave both of them. Scripture isn't just sweetness. It also contains the piercing light of God's holiness, righteousness, and purity—to keep us from sinning.

6. In Ezra 7:6–10, we read that Ezra was well-versed in the scriptures and that the king "granted

him all his request, according to the hand of the LORD his God upon him." God's blessing was on him indeed! The same can be our experience today.

7. In John 13:17, Jesus said the path to God's blessing is knowing *and doing* what God says. All the blessings of the Beatitudes (Matthew 5:3–12 and Luke 6:20–23) are ours, if only we obey the Lord and heed His Word.

8. In James 1:16–25 (NKJV), James said the person who does what God's Word says "will be blessed in what he does" (v. 25). He accepts the Bible as God's inspired Word, repents of his sins, humbly accepts the Word, experiences salvation, and then intently and continually looks into scripture and doesn't forget what he reads. Instead, he does what it says—and is blessed!

Pray:

Yes, Lord, I want to say "Thank You!" for motivating me to understand and apply Your Word in each area of my life.

More Insights on Inspiration
Read Jeremiah 36:1–19

Key Verse:

So Jeremiah sent for Baruch son of Neriah, and as Jeremiah dictated all the prophecies that the LORD had given him, Baruch wrote them on a scroll.
JEREMIAH 36:4 NLT

Understand:

- *What puzzles you about God-inspired scripture?*
- *What do you wish were different?*

Apply:

The book of Jeremiah offers more insights into God's inspiration of the Bible:

1. Inspiration begins the moment God reveals any portion of His truth to His prophets for His people (Jeremiah 36:1). Text is not inspired when it's recognized as canonical (accepted by the church). It's not even inspired when it's written. Instead, it's inspired the second God communicates it. The prophet knew immediately that he had received a new revelation from God. He didn't have to think twice about it!

2. Inspiration often begins as an oral message that the prophet or apostle dictates or pens. It's inspired

whether it's written down immediately or after an extended period of time (Jeremiah 36:1–2, 32). In this way, inspiration continues. It doesn't evaporate after God stops talking to a prophet or apostle.

3. Inspired messages communicate God's words to humanity in an exact form. They become inspired scriptures (writings) the moment they are penned. Their value as God's Word does *not* increase, but their effectiveness does. People can reconsider recorded messages and read them along with other messages from other times (Jeremiah 36:3).

4. Inspiration is not dependent on the written scriptures. When you share portions of scripture orally, you are transmitting God's Word to others (Jeremiah 36:9–16). In that way, you've become one of the links that helps God's Word become part of people's thoughts and actions.

There's more!

Pray:

Yes, Lord, I want to say "Thank You!" for all the ways You inspired the scriptures. It wasn't a static or boring process. Instead, it was a dynamic, active, and varied process. You worked through several dozen men to bless billions. Wow indeed!

Still More Insights on Inspiration
Read Jeremiah 36:20–32

Key Verse:

*Even though [they] urged the king not to burn
the scroll, he would not listen to them.*
JEREMIAH 36:25 NIV

Understand:

- *How do you think Jeremiah and Baruch
  felt about writing down God-inspired
  messages?*
- *What must have felt the most frustrating
  to them?*

Apply:

The book of Jeremiah offers still more insights into
God's inspiration of the Bible:

5. Verbal plenary inspiration does not depend on
the actual existence of the originals today (Jeremiah
36:32). Jeremiah dictated "all the former words that
were in the first scroll." He wrote a second scroll of
newly inspired scripture that a wicked king had tried
to destroy (36:22–23, 28).

6. Inspiration is progressive. Each book was
inspired one thought at a time. Often long gaps sep-
arated sections (Jeremiah 36:2, 32).

7. Inspiration is exclusively God's message to humanity, through human instruments and their secretaries (Jeremiah 36:4 and Romans 16:22).

8. Inspiration is always dependent on the Lord. Even though Jeremiah was a prophet of God, he couldn't prophesy whenever he felt like it. Sometimes the word of the Lord came to Jeremiah, compelling him to prophesy (Jeremiah 37:6). Sometimes the Lord gave Jeremiah a message as he spoke (37:17—this was essentially a message Jeremiah had delivered often before). Sometimes Jeremiah had to wait awhile until the Lord finally gave him a message (42:7).

9. Inspiration applies to the very choice of words. Jeremiah felt strongly that he had to deliver the whole message of the Lord, without omitting a word (Jeremiah 42:4 and 43:1). Jeremiah also wrote down his own thoughts and the remarks of others, but the Holy Spirit directed every word he wrote.

Pray:

Yes, Lord, I want to say "Thank You!" that wicked men couldn't destroy even one passage of Your eternal Word.

The Biblical Heroes
Moses and Joshua
Read Joshua 8:30–35

Key Verse:

*There was not a word of all that Moses had commanded
that Joshua did not read to the whole assembly of
Israel, including the women and children,
and the foreigners who lived among them.*
JOSHUA 8:35 NIV

Understand:

- *Have you ever heard someone question
  the reliability of the Bible's first book,
  Genesis?*
- *What assumptions do such critics and
  skeptics make?*

Apply:

It's common to wonder, *Do we have all the right books
in God's Word?* You can know for sure over these next
few days of Bible study.

The first books of the Bible reveal the preservation of scripture from generation to generation.

The Books of Moses. The first five books of the Bible weren't put away in some obscure place after Moses wrote them. God gave Moses and the Israelites careful instructions during the latter part of Moses' life for the care and regular reading of the Law before "all Israel" (Deuteronomy 31:9–13, 24–29).

By the time Joshua found himself leading the Israelite nation, he recognized Genesis through Deuteronomy as written by Moses through God's direction (Joshua 1:8–9). Joshua probably had possession of the original writings.

Scribes made fastidious copies of the original autographs (with word-for-word precision), and God's people considered these equally authoritative (Joshua 8:32–35 and Deuteronomy 27:3, 8). Verbal transmission was also authoritative (Joshua 8:34–35).

The Book of Joshua. Joshua wrote his book soon after the events recorded in it occurred. Records of what God told him suggest this. Specific historical references date the book to the time of Joshua, certainly much earlier than 1000 BC (see Joshua 15:63 and 16:10). Writers later added other authoritative material to Joshua's records. This includes material added soon after his death (Joshua 15:13–19 and 24:29–33), when the records were being collected and probably copied in more permanent form.

Pray:

Yes, Lord, I want to say "Thank You!" that everything Moses and Joshua wrote in the first six books of the Bible is still in my hands today.

Ezra Preserves the Hebrew Scriptures

Read Ezra 7:11–26

Key Verse:

"And you, Ezra, according to the wisdom of your God that is in your hand, appoint magistrates and judges who may judge all the people in the province Beyond the River, all such as know the laws of your God. And those who do not know them, you shall teach."

 EZRA 7:25 ESV

Understand:

- *Did you notice how the king described Ezra in verses 11, 12, and 21? Why is this significant?*
- *In verses 14 and 25, what does the king say is in Ezra's possession? Why is this so important?*

Apply:

When all is said and done, God's people have all the right books in the Old Testament. Tradition says Ezra wrote part of the Old Testament himself and helped confirm much of the Old Testament canon— the books the Jewish people believed God spoke through the prophets. This canon was started before

1400 BC (the books of Moses) and completed after 450 BC (Malachi).

According to first-century Jewish historian Josephus, the Jewish people divided the Old Testament into the following sections:

- The Books of Moses: Genesis, Exodus, Leviticus, Numbers, Deuteronomy.
- The Prophets: Joshua, Ruth and Judges (considered one book), Samuel, Kings, Isaiah, Jeremiah and Lamentations (one book), Ezekiel, the twelve Minor Prophets (one book), Daniel, Job, Esther, Ezra and Nehemiah (one book), and Chronicles.
- The Writings: Psalms, Proverbs, Song of Solomon, and Ecclesiastes. Sometimes Job, Ruth and Judges, Lamentations, Esther, Daniel, Ezra and Nehemiah, and Chronicles were added to this third section of writings.

Well over two millennia later, God's people still have every book of the Old Testament intact and in hand. That's amazing!

Pray:

Yes, Lord, I want to say "Thank You!" for making sure we have had every book of the Old Testament for thousands of years.

Scribes Preserved God's Word
Read Ezra 7:1–10

Key Verse:

*For Ezra had set his heart to study the Law
of the LORD, and to do it and to teach
his statutes and rules in Israel.*
EZRA 7:10 ESV

Understand:

- *Do you remember the telephone game? If
  so, why was it sometimes humorous?*
- *How similar or different is the story of
  the Bible's transmission down through
  the ages?*

Apply:

It's common to ask, "Does every verse in scripture
say what it's supposed to say?" Thankfully, textual
criticism plays an important role in confirming the
inspiration of scripture.

Textual criticism is a careful science that uses
thousands of ancient manuscripts to determine texts
that are most like the original copies. None of the
manuscripts considered are originals (since they have
long since been lost or destroyed), so the reliability of
the copies must be proved. God's people can be sure

of the accuracy of the transmission of the original message to the copies in several ways.

First, after the Babylonian Captivity, Ezra and other scribes carefully went to work to ensure that plenty of copies of God's Word would always exist. These scribes became known as "lawyers" because of their knowledge of the Old Testament law.

Second, the Talmudists (AD 100–450), the Masoretes (AD 450–900), and other such groups who copied under the strictest of rules, reproduced the Old Testament. Their high standards reflect the accuracy of their copying. Here are only two of the many rules they followed:

- They could not correct the original if they felt it was wrong (they could only add notations in the margins).
- On each line they copied, they counted the number of letters and words, compared middle words, checked the frequency of each letter, and the like.

There's more!

Pray:

Yes, Lord, I want to say "Thank You!" for the incredible work done by scribes to preserve the scriptures down through the ages. May I never take the Bible for granted again.

More about the Scribes
Read Malachi 4:1-6

Key Verse:

*"Remember to obey the Law of Moses, my servant—
all the decrees and regulations that I gave
him on Mount Sinai for all Israel."*
MALACHI 4:4 NLT

Understand:

- *Some Bibles use the word Savior
  and some use Saviour. What are the
  differences in meaning?*
- *The original King James Version uses the
  word "let" in the sense of "hinder." What's
  changed in the past four hundred years? The
  accuracy of the Bible—or something else?*

Apply:

Here are several more rules that the Talmudists,
Masoretes, and others followed when copying the
Old Testament scriptures:

- They could not copy from memory.
- They used the space of a hair between
  each letter. (Talk about precise!)
- They reverently burned or buried old,

worn copies of scripture (to avoid profaning the Lord's name, should they become smudged or otherwise unreadable).

How accurate were these scribes? Bible scholars familiar with their work confidently assert that the time gap doesn't mean the text has degenerated over the millennia. In his *Survey of the Bible*, William Hendriksen quotes one scholar who said, "If we had in our possession a first- or second-century manuscript, we would find it to have substantially the same text as those of much later date."

Only months after that statement was published, the Dead Sea Scrolls were discovered in a cave in Qumran. Among the findings were two copies of the book of Isaiah dating back to 150 BC. Hebrew scholars diligently compared the newly discovered manuscripts with much more recent manuscripts that had come from the Masoretic tradition and were dated from the medieval period. Their conclusion? Only a few insignificant changes (mostly spelling variations) had crept into the Isaiah text after more than a millennium!

Thanks to the careful work of the Jewish scribes, we can rest assured that the Old Testament has been passed on to us with a very high degree of accuracy. Wow indeed!

Pray:

Yes, Lord, I want to say "Wow!" for the incredible accuracy of the Old Testament scriptures preserved for all of history.

The New Testament's Reliability
Read Luke 1:1–25

Key Verse:

Having carefully investigated everything from the beginning, I also have decided to write an accurate account for you, most honorable Theophilus.
LUKE 1:3 NLT

Understand:

- *Which do you think are more reliable: the writings of Plato, Aristotle, and Homer—or the New Testament's twenty-seven books?*
- *Is it even close?*

Apply:

There is an overwhelming amount of evidence for the accuracy of the New Testament. Men wrote its twenty-seven books between AD 40 and 100. The earliest known copy of part of the New Testament is dated only a few short decades after the completion of the original.

Also, there are 5,400 ancient copies of the New Testament in Greek, 10,000 more in Latin, and 9,300 more in other languages. From this wealth of sources, scholars and experts have made comparisons to accurately determine the original.

Sir Frederic George Kenyon, former director and principal librarian of the British Museum, said, "Thanks to these manuscripts, the ordinary reader of the Bible may feel comfortable about the soundness of the text. Apart from a few unimportant verbal alterations, natural in books transcribed by hand, the New Testament, we now feel assured, has come down intact."

What's more, almost the entire New Testament can be reproduced from the writings of the second- and third-century church fathers alone. All but eleven verses can be reconstructed from the verses they cited.

In sharp contrast, other classical writings are suspect at best. Scholars have only seven copies of Plato's writings, dating 1,200 years after his death. They have only five copies of Aristotle's writings, dating 1,400 years after his death. They have 643 copies of Homer's writings, dating 1,800 years after his death, with errors prevalent in 5 percent of his 15,600 lines.

You can read every section of the New Testament with confidence!

Pray:

Yes, Lord, I want to say "Wow!" for the incredible accuracy of the New Testament scriptures. I can read and study Your Word with incredible confidence.

The Church Preserves
the New Testament
Read Acts 1:1–26

Key Verse:

*In my former book, Theophilus, I wrote about
all that Jesus began to do and to teach.*
ACTS 1:1 NIV

Understand:

- *Tradition says Luke wrote the book of
  Acts in anticipation of Paul's trial before
  Caesar. What does Luke say in Acts that
  seems to confirm this?*
- *The name Theophilus means "friend of
  God." Do you think he was a real person?
  Why or why not?*

Apply:

Soon after the church began, the need for a second
canon of accepted scripture writings developed. The
New Testament canon formed much more quickly
than the Old Testament because of the loss of the
apostles and other witnesses, the expansion of Christianity beyond Palestine, the need to protect the Message from false teachings, the persecution of believers
(they needed to know which books they would die

for), and the missionary enterprise (they needed to know which books to translate and use in preaching).

The early church went through several steps to finalize the New Testament canon. Most of the books were widely recognized as canonical in the second and third centuries. Some seriously questioned only a few of the latter books in the New Testament. By AD 397, two official church councils had confirmed the canonical nature of the twenty-seven books of the New Testament.

Members of these councils asked specific questions to determine which books were canonical:

- Is it written by or under the direction of an apostle?
- Is it inspired by the Holy Spirit?
- Is it circulated among the churches?
- Is it consistent with the rest of scripture?

Some reliable books were left out of the canon, including a Harmony of the Four Gospels. It was widely read among the churches, but didn't measure up to the four rigid standards of canonicity. Many unreliable books were rejected out of hand.

How good to know Christians have all the right books in the New Testament!

Pray:

Yes, Lord, I want to say "Thank You!" for inspiring Matthew, Mark, Luke, John, Peter, James, Jude, and Paul to write the New Testament scriptures. It was hard work, but they preserved it.

Nothing Lost in Translation
Read 2 Timothy 3:10–17

Key Verse:

You have been taught the holy Scriptures from childhood, and they have given you the wisdom to receive the salvation that comes by trusting in Christ Jesus.
2 Timothy 3:15 nlt

Understand:

- *Have you ever found a typographical error in one of your Bibles? If so, what does it mean?*
- *And, what does that typo not mean?*

Apply:

It's common to ask, "What about translations? What's lost in some of them?" Thankfully, the apostle Paul gave us the biblical perspective we should have toward copies and translations.

The scripture Paul referred to as "inspired by God" was not a collection of the original works. It was only one among thousands of copies of the Old Testament scriptures. Additionally, these scriptures were translated from Hebrew and Aramaic into Greek (a translation known as the Septuagint).

Without hesitation, Paul told Timothy that the sacred writings he had known from childhood were able to give him wisdom leading to salvation. Then he added: "All Scripture is God-breathed and is useful for teaching, rebuking, correcting and training in righteousness, so that the servant of God may be thoroughly equipped for every good work" (2 Timothy 3:16–17 NIV).

Because of this, we can see that copies and translated works are still inspired. They accurately reflect the original manuscripts and communicate God's intended meaning.

The verdict?

Our English Bibles truly *are* inspired. They are the Word of God communicated to us in a language we can read, understand, personalize, and apply to our lives.

Pray:

Yes, Lord, I want to say "Thank You!" again for
motivating me to go through this book and learn
so much about how to read and study
and apply Your Word to my life.

The Reliability of Translations
Read 2 Timothy 2:1–15

Key Verse:

Do your best to present yourself to God as one approved, a worker who has no need to be ashamed, rightly handling the word of truth.
2 Timothy 2:15 esv

Understand:

- *Do you think Jesus and the apostles ever read, studied, and memorized Bible verses translated from Hebrew into Greek?*
- *What would it mean if they had?*

Apply:

Throughout the ages, God's people have accepted, valued, created, and used Bible translations to reach the widest possible audiences.

How do you know that Bible translations are trustworthy? Here are four reasons:

1. The apostle Paul affirmed the inspiration of Bible translations (2 Timothy 3:14–17). Paul spoke Hebrew fluently. Still, to effectively communicate to his listeners and readers, he often quoted from the Greek translation of the Old Testament (Acts 13:34, Romans 9:12, 1 Corinthians 2:9).

2. The apostle Peter affirmed the inspiration of Bible translations (2 Peter 1:19–21). Peter probably spoke all three of the original languages of the Bible. Because the Greek translation of the Old Testament was popular in his day, he often quoted from it (Acts 2:17–21 and 3:22).

3. Jesus Himself affirmed the eternal nature of the Bible (Matthew 5:17–18), exemplified God's great love for the whole world (John 3:16 and 17:20), and often quoted from the Greek translation of the Old Testament (Matthew 9:13, Mark 14:27, Luke 4:12, and John 15:25).

4. The apostle John affirmed the eternal nature of the Bible (Revelation 22:18–19), proclaimed God's great love for the whole world (1 John 2:2), and often quoted from the Greek translation of the Old Testament (John 12:38 and 19:36–37).

There's more!

Pray:

Yes, Lord, I want to say "Thank You!" that I don't have to be ashamed about how I rightly handle the Word of Truth. May I sense Your blessing and approval today.

More on the Reliability of Translations
Read 2 Timothy 1:1–14

Key Verse:

Through the power of the Holy Spirit who lives within us, carefully guard the precious truth that has been entrusted to you.

2 TIMOTHY 1:14 NLT

Understand:

- *Within your extended family tree, going back as far as you can, how many languages were spoken? One? Two? Three?*
- *Within your family today, how many languages are spoken?*

Apply:

Here are four more reasons you can be certain that Bible translations are trustworthy:

5. The apostle Matthew is the only New Testament writer who apparently didn't quote from the Greek translation of the Old Testament. That's because his original audience was predominately Jewish.

6. The early church produced a number of important translations of the Old and New Testaments during the first four centuries after Jesus

Christ's ascension: Old Latin, Latin, Syriac, Coptic, Old Nubian, Armenian, Old Georgian, Ethiopic, and Gothic. They used these translations to reach as many people as possible with God's Word. New Christians weren't forced to learn the original Bible languages.

7. To help fulfill Jesus Christ's Great Commission, the church has now translated the Bible or portions of the Bible into more than 2,200 languages. Why? Because less than 0.00001 percent of the people alive today understand the three ancient biblical languages, and more than 85 percent don't understand English fluently. The scriptures are best understood when translated into the reader's (or listener's) native language.

8. Every significant English Bible published within the past generation or two has been translated by an interdenominational team of scores of scholars working from the Hebrew, Aramaic, and Greek texts. They're aided by contemporary literary consultants and by a library of scholarship compiled over the past few centuries.

Pray:

Yes, Lord, I want to say "Thank You!" that I can read my English Bible with confidence in its trustworthiness and sacred truths.

The Rules of Translation
Read John 19:17–22

Key Verse:

Many of the Jews read this inscription, for the place where Jesus was crucified was near the city, and it was written in Aramaic, in Latin, and in Greek.
JOHN 19:20 ESV

Understand:

- *Do some, many, or all of your favorite sports have carefully articulated rules?*
- *When it comes to Bible translation, why are rules even more important?*

Apply:

Again, almost all Bible translations are trustworthy. That's true in almost every language. Wycliffe Bible Translators has used the following rules for its work around the world:

Based on the best Hebrew and Greek texts. English isn't good enough.

Other than word-for-word. Martin Luther put it this way: "What do the Germans say in such a situation?" In other words, how would the man on the street say it in plain German?

Fastidious in meaning or form. The Living Bible's

paraphrase of Revelation 18:22 says, "Never again will the sound of music be there—no more pianos, saxophones, and trumpets." Many translators would agree that particular paraphrase crosses the line between biblical facts and sanctified imagination.

Structurally adapted to maintain accuracy. In a number of languages within the Philippines, for example, the phrase "verily, verily" or "truly, truly" is best translated as one word, not two.

Updated regularly as language changes. In the King James Version, 1 Thessalonians 4:15 uses an archaic form of the verb *prevent.* Instead, modern translations use the current form of the verb *precede* to ensure that readers know what Paul is really saying.

Free from any theological biases. The New World Translation twists John 1:1 to say—counter to all grammatical rules in Greek—that Jesus was merely "a god," not God Himself. That's a blatant mistranslation of a key verse in scripture. Thankfully, virtually all major English Bibles are free from such theological errors.

Pray:

*Yes, Lord, I want to say "Thank You!" that the Bible
or portions of the Bible have been translated into
thousands of languages around the world.
Almost everyone I know and meet can
read Your Word in his mother tongue.*

Questionable Translations
Read 2 Peter 3:1–18

Key Verse:

*His [Paul's] letters contain some things that are hard to
understand, which ignorant and unstable people distort,
as they do the other Scriptures, to their own destruction.*
2 PETER 3:16 NIV

Understand:

- *Imagine two Mormons come to your door.
  You offer to read their literature if they read
  the letter to the Romans and then come
  back. How do you think they will respond?*
- *Imagine two Jehovah's Witnesses come to
  your door. You want to study the Gospel of
  John with them. Which Bible translation
  do you think you should use?*

Apply:

We don't need to worry about questionable English
Bible translations. This may sound counterintuitive,
but it's true. Here are four reasons why:

1. They're often the product of an individual,
small group, or cult.

2. They're rarely available for sale in Christian
bookstores.

3. These questionable translations still contain God's Word. Except for verses in which the translators twisted scripture (say, John 1:1 in the New World Translation), you could read these translations with benefit. While that's not recommended, these translations are still well over ninety-five percent the inspired Word of God. However, this doesn't excuse the scripture-twisting the translators did in some places.

4. These translations are often highly revered but little read. Many members of these religious communities memorize specific scriptures and do their prescribed Bible studies each week, but they don't actually read the Bible like a book, cover to cover.

So the next time two cult members come knocking on your door, don't be afraid to discuss the scriptures with them. Ask them to open up their Bibles right on the spot. Don't be afraid to read over their shoulders, so to speak. Their questionable Bible translation isn't going to hurt you!

Pray that God will reveal Himself to these individuals through His Word, despite known translation errors.

Pray:

Yes, Lord, I want to say "Thank You!" for this new perspective on using Your Word to reach the men who knock on my door representing unorthodox groups.

God Has Protected His Word

Read Psalm 119:89–105

Key Verse:

Forever, O LORD,
your word is firmly fixed in the heavens.
PSALM 119:89 ESV

Understand:

- *If the Lord could but speak and create the entire universe, is anything too hard for Him?*
- *What about safeguarding the Bible in human hands here on earth?*

Apply:

God has carefully protected the Bible. How do we know that? Here are eight reasons:

1. God Himself promises that scripture is completely true and trustworthy (Psalms 19:7, 33:4 and 119:42). He wants us to take it seriously!

2. Today's key verse affirms that scripture is eternal (Psalm 119:89). Unlike the world's fads, which come and go, God's Word has endured the test of time.

3. The greatest Old Testament prophet after Moses and a leading apostle of Jesus Christ both affirmed that scripture stands forever (Isaiah 40:8 and 1 Peter 1:23–25).

4. Jesus Himself promised that scripture will remain until its purpose is achieved (Matthew 5:18). Nothing will be lost before the end of time.

5. The first prophet and the last apostle both issued harsh warnings to anyone who dared tamper with scripture (Deuteronomy 4:2 and Revelation 22:18–19; see also Proverbs 30:6).

6. The discovery of the Dead Sea Scrolls confirms the remarkable accuracy of the transmission of the Old Testament over thousands of years.

7. The wealth of manuscripts dating back to the first century AD confirms the text of the New Testament beyond any shadow of a doubt.

8. Every critic's claim to have found a supposed "error" in scripture has been discredited without exception for the past four centuries. That's a remarkable track record!

Pray:

Yes, Lord, I want to say "Thank You!" that You have protected Your Word and still use it with great power and effectiveness today.

The Bible's Selective Reporting
Read John 20:30–21:25

Key Verse:

Jesus performed many other signs in the presence of his disciples, which are not recorded in this book.
JOHN 20:30 NIV

Understand:

- *Imagine the Yankees and Red Sox just split a doubleheader. How similarly or differently will the games be reported in Boston and New York?*
- *Imagine the Seahawks just beat the 49ers with a last-second field goal. How will the news differ up and down the West Coast?*

Apply:

When it comes to addressing apparent Bible contradictions, perhaps it would be best to start with the basic principles of journalism. These include seeking answers to six key journalism questions: *Who? What? When? Where? Why?* and *How?*

Any journalist worth his salt will compile far more facts than can be reported in an article and then use the principle of selectivity to report only the facts deemed most relevant to the intended readers. As a result, a news story about an NBA game will sound far different in the guest team's hometown than in the home team's. Same game, same hundreds or thousands of facts—but a different audience!

The same principle of selectivity applies to scripture. Moses didn't write down everything that happened in Adam's life. Far from it. He recorded only what God said was relevant.

The same is true when John wrote his Gospel. He wasn't trying to write *The Exhaustive Life of Jesus Christ.* Instead, he admitted, "Jesus did many other things as well. If every one of them were written down, I suppose that even the whole world would not have room for the books that would be written" (John 21:25 niv).

In other words, John selected only those events, miracles, interviews, teachings, prayers, persecutions, and sufferings that best communicated the Gospel message to his intended audience. The other three Gospel writers did the same. All the better for us!

Pray:

Yes, Lord, I want to say "Thank You!" for how professional sports help me better understand the selective reporting of the biblical writers.

Presuppositions for Studying Apparent Errors

Read Colossians 2:1–23

Key Verse:

*See to it that no one takes you captive through hollow
and deceptive philosophy, which depends on human
tradition and the elemental spiritual forces
of this world rather than on Christ.*

Colossians 2:8 niv

Understand:

- *One in five Americans tell pollsters that
  they are skeptical or hostile toward the
  Bible. When asked if the Bible contains
  errors, they say, "Yes!"*
- *What percentage of these individuals do
  you think has carefully and objectively
  studied five or more apparent Bible
  errors?*

Apply:

Our English Bibles are *very* accurate. God has carefully preserved the scriptures down through the ages.
We can read and study God's Word with the utmost
confidence that it *is* still God's message for us today.

Before tackling an apparent "error" in scripture,

it's important to think through one's basic assumptions about the reliability of the Bible. The following presuppositions should form the grid through which you study potential biblical mistakes:

1. Some apparent errors were caused by faulty transmission or translation of scripture.

2. Some apparent errors are caused by faulty observations or interpretations of scripture.

3. Most apparent errors can be solved by discovering the source of the problem and examining it carefully and honestly.

4. Some apparent errors will be fully solved only when further information is available.

5. We must reserve judgment on apparent errors we can't solve because of our limited knowledge, recognizing that it is always wiser to depend on God's Word than to trust the words of mere men.

Pray:

Yes, Lord, I want to say "Thank You!" for these five presuppositions, which eliminate any fear I might have about potential Bible errors.

Process for Studying
Potential Errors
Read 2 Thessalonians 2:1–17

Key Verse:

*Now may our Lord Jesus Christ himself, and God
our Father, who loved us and gave us eternal comfort
and good hope through grace, comfort your hearts and
establish them in every good work and word.*
2 THESSALONIANS 2:16–17 ESV

Understand:

- *Did you know that quotation marks
  weren't invented until the 1400s and
  weren't used to denote quoted material
  until the 1600s?*
- *So, what do quotation marks mean—and
  not mean—when used in our English
  Bibles?*

Apply:

When you're doing your daily Bible reading and
studying, an apparent "error" may trigger a red light
in your thinking. Rather than ignoring it, discover
if there's really a problem. Simply use this six-step
process:

1. Identify the scripture passage(s).

2. Define the problem in the passage(s).
3. Classify the "error:"

- contradiction in parallel accounts
- mistake in historical detail
- problem in scientific description
- inconsistency in moral teaching

4. Examine possible sources for the "error:"

- faulty transmission (did a scribal error occur?)
- faulty translation (do contemporary versions differ?)
- faulty observation (have you carefully examined the text and context?)
- faulty interpretation (have you understood this passage correctly?)

5. Identify the possible source of the problem.
6. Suggest a tentative answer to the problem.

Pray:

Yes, Lord, I want to say "Thank You!" for this six-step process for dealing with apparent errors in the Bible. I already feel more at peace.

Studying the Bible's "Toughest Error"
Read John 18:15–27

Key Verse:

The servant girl at the door said to Peter, "You also are not one of this man's disciples, are you?" He said, "I am not."
JOHN 18:17 ESV

Understand:

- *Which woman or women went to the tomb of Jesus early that Sunday morning? Mary Magdalene (John 20:1)? Her and "the other Mary" (Matthew 28:1)? Both Marys and Salome (Mark 16:1)? Both Marys and Joanna and "other women" (Luke 24:10)?*
- *Are all our accounts correct? Why or why not?*

Apply:

One of the few things all four Gospels record is Peter's three denials the night before Jesus' crucifixion (Matthew 26:69–75, Mark 14:66–71, Luke 22:55–62, and John 18:16–27). But to whom did Peter deny the Lord? The four Gospel writers give differing accounts. Do their differences contradict each other?

Like a good journalist, each Gospel writer had a specific purpose for writing his account. He had a specific audience in mind. By definition, he had to leave out most of what he knew (otherwise, he never would have finished writing!). Leaving out secondary and tertiary details isn't wrong—it's what *every* good writer does.

Actually, their differences don't contradict—they *complement* each other.

So to whom did Peter deny Jesus Christ? Any good journalist can harmonize the four Gospel accounts rather easily:

- First denial: one maid who talked to a second maid about Peter
- Second denial: the two maids plus others who confronted Peter
- Third denial: a larger group of bystanders, including a servant who was upset with Peter

Bottom line: Over the years, critics have cited Peter's three denials as the "ultimate proof" that the Bible contains errors. Their adamant remarks, however, aren't backed up by the actual scriptural accounts.

Pray:

Yes, Lord, I want to say "Thank You!" again that professional sports reporting helps me quickly and easily resolve differing accounts within the four Gospels.

Harmony in the Old Testament
Read Exodus 24:1–18

Key Verse:

Moses then wrote down everything the LORD had said.
EXODUS 24:4 NIV

Understand:

- *What swallowed the prophet Jonah? A "whale" (Matthew 12:40 KJV) or a "great fish" (Jonah 1:17 KJV)?*
- *Using the Bible(s) you have, how quickly can you determine the correct answer?*

Apply:

Critics and skeptics haven't just had a heyday with apparent contradictions regarding Peter's three denials. They've also cited apparent contradictions in other parallel accounts, including these examples:

- Who incited King David to number the people (2 Samuel 24:1 vs. 1 Chronicles 21:1)
- Who killed Goliath (1 Samuel 17:49–51 and 21:9 vs. 2 Samuel 21:19)
- Who owned the threshing floor (2 Samuel 6:6 vs. 1 Chronicles 13:9)

- Which city King David captured
  (2 Samuel 8:1 vs. 1 Chronicles 18:1)
- How many enemies were killed (2
  Samuel 23:8 vs. 1 Chronicles 11:11)
- How much King David paid (2 Samuel
  24:24 vs. 1 Chronicles 21:24–25)

Thankfully, all of these problems are easily resolved.

In years gone by, critics also argued that the Bible contains historical errors. They claimed scripture wrongly attributes the authorship of Genesis through Deuteronomy to Moses, "even though writing wasn't invented until after his death." Scholars, however, have long since proved the critics wrong. These scholars can point to more than half a dozen written languages that extend back before the time of Moses.

Pray:

Yes, Lord, I want to say "Thank You!" that this also applies when I read differing accounts in the Hebrew scriptures. I'll never look at professional sports reporting the same again.

The Bible Is Rooted in History
Read Acts 2:14–41

Key Verse:

"Let all the house of Israel therefore know for certain that God has made him both Lord and Christ, this Jesus whom you crucified."
ACTS 2:36 ESV

Understand:

- *After His resurrection, Jesus appeared to His disciples for forty days and then ascended back to heaven. Their initial fear gave way to boldness and courage rarely seen in human history. What made such a radical change in their hearts and minds?*
- *Ten days after Jesus ascended, Peter boldly preached the Gospel to thousands of people. To what did he appeal? To the Hebrew scriptures, yes. What else?*

Apply:

The biblical writers often took the time to describe the historical accuracy of their writings. Here are a few brief examples from the New Testament:

- John verified the actual physical death of Jesus Christ by reminding his readers that he was an eyewitness of Jesus' final moments on the cross (John 19:34–35).

- Peter appealed to the knowledge of the crowd when he talked about Jesus on the Day of Pentecost (Acts 2:22). If he was fabricating a story, he would have received a far different response at the end of his sermon.
- Paul appealed to the knowledge of King Agrippa as he talked about Jesus Christ (Acts 26:26). Jesus Christ and His disciples hadn't performed miracles in some obscure corner—everyone knew about them.
- Paul said that to deny the possibility of someone's rising from the dead was to deny the obvious historical fact of Jesus Christ's resurrection (1 Corinthians 15:1–8).
- Peter rightfully claimed to have been an eyewitness of one of Jesus Christ's most glorious miracles—the Transfiguration (2 Peter 1:16–18).
- John reminded the early Christians toward the end of the first century that he and others had repeatedly touched Jesus Christ (1 John 1:1–3).

Pray:

Yes, Lord, I want to say "Thank You!" that Judaism and Christianity are rooted in history, unlike other religions.

The Bible and Science
Read Romans 1:16–23

Key Verse:

For since the creation of the world God's invisible qualities—his eternal power and divine nature—have been clearly seen, being understood from what has been made, so that people are without excuse.
ROMANS 1:20 NIV

Understand:

- *Did you know that the ancient Chinese, Indians, Mesopotamians, Babylonians, Egyptians, Greeks, and Romans celebrated (and sometimes weaponized) scientific discoveries?*
- *Did you know these ancient civilizations developed the empirical (scientific) method, geometry, advanced mathematics, astronomy, atomism, deductive reasoning, physics, and much more?*

Apply:

Some critics have argued that the Bible contains scientific errors. They claim scripture incorrectly speaks of the sun "going down" (see Ephesians 4:26). They gleefully point out that Galileo discredited this concept centuries ago. Despite the critics' claims, however, the idea of the sun "going down" is still part of the English language. Almost everyone loves to watch a spectacular sunrise or sunset. Every day news agencies across the country list the times for the sun to come up and go down.

Other scientific "problems" include these two false ideas:

1. The Bible can't be proven scientifically. The problem is a matter of confusion on the part of the critics. The scientific method is a very limited test. It can't prove historical facts (Abraham Lincoln was president of the United States), musical standards (Mozart was a brilliant composer), tenets of faith (Jesus Christ is God's Son), or matters of the heart (you love your family).

2. The uniformity of nature makes supernatural intervention (miracles) impossible. Of course these critics are leaving God out of their picture! If God *is* God, He can do whatever He wants—even supersede the principles governing His creation. Besides, the scientific theory of the universe as an absolutely uniform system is more than half a century out of date.

Pray:

Yes, Lord, I want to say "Thank You!" that the Bible's supposed scientific errors are themselves in error. Yes, I know the Bible isn't a science textbook. I know it uses figures of speech. Still, I can trust it cover to cover.

The Bible's Harmony with Science
Read Psalm 19:1–6

Key Verse:

*The heavens declare the glory of God,
and the sky above proclaims his handiwork.*
PSALM 19:1 ESV

Understand:

- *Scientific discoveries birth more discoveries. Sometimes, new discoveries correct faulty ideas. Is this good or bad?*
- *We still don't know how many hundreds of billions of stars are in our galaxy alone. Estimates vary by up to a third of a trillion stars. Is this good or bad?*

Apply:

Even though the Bible isn't a science textbook, its scientific descriptions contain no real problems. In fact, many of its statements, though contrary to scientific thought at the time, have long since been proven true. Here are four examples:

1. Many hundreds of years before the theory of the circulation of blood within the body was even proposed, the Bible proclaimed that life is in our blood (Genesis 9:4).

2. Ancient civilizations commonly believed the earth was held in place by some support such as a large reptile's back or a set of pillars. But Job 26:7 declares, "He [God] stretches out the north over empty space; He hangs the earth on nothing."

3. The Greek astronomer Hipparchus (c. 190–120 BC) confidently stated, "There are only 1,056 stars in the heavens. I have counted them." In the second century AD, Ptolemy counted 1,056 and agreed that no others existed. Yet Jeremiah 33:22 insists, "The host [stars] of heaven cannot be numbered." Not until AD 1610 did Galileo look through a telescope and prove the Bible right.

4. On a clear night, many of the stars that appear in the sky look alike. Modern astronomers have photographed millions, however, and found no two are identical. Paul spoke about this nearly 2,000 years ago: "One star differs from another star in glory" (1 Corinthians 15:41).

Pray:

Yes, Lord, I want to say "Thank You!" for reminding me that the Bible is in harmony with important scientific truths.

The Bible's Clear Morality
Read Jude 1:1–25

Key Verse:

But these people scoff at things they do not understand. Like unthinking animals, they do whatever their instincts tell them, and so they bring about their own destruction.
JUDE 1:10 NLT

Understand:

- *Early Christians were often martyred for their unbending faith in Jesus Christ. Was this good or bad?*
- *Then again, few early Christians were willing to be martyred in protest of infanticide, let alone gladiator fights to the death and other gruesome blood sports. Was this good or bad?*

Apply:

Some critics have argued that the Bible contains moral errors. They claim that Jesus and His disciples violated one of the Ten Commandments by working on the Sabbath. Did they? In Matthew 12:1–2, the Pharisees emphatically said yes. According to their list of rules, someone was "working" if he walked through a field when the heads of grain were mature. Yet their rule went far beyond anything the Old Testament actually said. In fact, Deuteronomy 23:25 says someone could pick grain from someone else's field if he was hungry. Jesus said He came to fulfill the law (Matthew 5:17), but He had little patience for those who oppressed the multitudes with all their man-made regulations.

Other moral "problems" include these two dubious criticisms:

1. The Bible is full of sex and violence. It's true that the Bible doesn't gloss over the violent and sometimes lustful lives of the people it mentions. Yet the Bible's purpose isn't to provide crude entertainment but to provide clear examples of what honors God—and what doesn't.

2. The Bible is often offensive. It's true that the Bible speaks of God's ultimate judgment against wrongdoers and provides many examples of His judgment here on earth. The real moral problem, however, resides not with the Lord or His Word but with those who would set themselves up as judges of either.

Pray:

Yes, Lord, I want to say "Thank You!" for the intrinsic, bedrock morality of Your Word, which reminds me daily of Your absolute holiness, righteousness, and justice.

How to Handle Doubts
Read 1 John 2:1–3:3

Key Verse:

*I write to you, not because you do not know
the truth, but because you know it,
and because no lie is of the truth.*

1 JOHN 2:21 ESV

Understand:

- *Jesus and the apostles recognized that
  men naturally have doubts. What is the
  opposite of doubt?*
- *What else is the opposite of doubt?*

Apply:

If left unaddressed, doubts will fester in your soul
and can lead to a lack of faith or outright unbelief. So
whatever you do, you can't ignore doubts!

Instead, here's how to handle them:

Revelation. You have to get back to the question,
How do you know what you believe? The answer is
that God has revealed His message in a book called
the Bible. In this book you find all the answers you
need for life and godliness. You don't find answers
to all of life's tough questions. But most of them are
answered with far greater authority and clarity than

thousands of years of philosophy has provided.

Authority. You have to address the question, *Who decides what is true?* Ultimately, the answer is God. He has stated His position quite clearly in the scriptures. God's Word is our absolute authority for faith and practice.

Inspiration. You have to tackle the question, *Is scripture inspired by God?* Scripture itself says yes. The early church fathers agreed. They also believed the Bible contained a unified message and story.

Doctrine. You have to wrestle with the question, *What do you believe?* The answer is in the teachings of your particular denomination or church. To the degree that they're based solidly on scripture, you can bank on them. The answer is also found in your own beliefs and convictions—and questions and doubts.

Pray:

Yes, Lord, I want to say "Thank You!" for this new perspective on doubts. I'm glad that having doubts is a good thing. Thanks too for showing me how to handle them.

Doubts Abound in a Fallen World
Read Mark 9:14–32

Key Verse:

*Immediately the boy's father exclaimed,
"I do believe; help me overcome my unbelief!"*
Mark 9:24 NIV

Understand:

- *What happens when you try to bury your
  doubts?*
- *What else happens?*

Apply:

Even the godliest Christian men struggle with
doubts. Doubts are a natural by-product of taking
God's Word seriously while living in a fallen world.

You need to bring your toughest questions to
the Lord. Scripture makes it clear that Jesus can
remove people's doubts (Matthew 14:25–31 and
Luke 24:36–45).

Where do doubts come from? Here are five
possibilities:

- Life has been very painful for you.
- You wonder if something scripture
  says is too good to be true.

- You have an incorrect perception of God or scripture.
- You have been introduced to false ideas.
- You are struggling with depression.

How do you get rid of doubts? Here are seven possibilities:

- Tell God about what has happened.
- Ask God to search your heart.
- Read scripture and study what it says.
- Affirm what you believe, obey, and heed.
- Ask the Lord to speak to your heart as you read and pray.
- Ask God to fill you with the Holy Spirit and teach you.
- Talk with someone you respect for his faith.

It's not a sin to have doubts—everyone has them. Don't pretend you don't. And whatever you do, don't hide them. Instead, deal with your doubts head-on. Address each one that comes up. In the end, your faith will be stronger!

Pray:

Yes, Lord, I want to say "Thank You!" for relieving my concerns about the doubts I have had. Please help me address and remove any doubts I have in the days ahead.

The Lord Loves Questions
Read Luke 2:39–52

Key Verse:

*Three days later they finally discovered him [Jesus]
in the Temple, sitting among the religious teachers,
listening to them and asking questions.*
LUKE 2:46 NLT

Understand:

- *What are the benefits of asking questions?*
- *What are the benefits of getting solid
  answers to our questions?*

Apply:

When you study the Bible, you want to be fully
engaged—mind, will, and emotions. Bible study
doesn't mean blind or passive acceptance of what
scripture says. Just the opposite!

Whatever you do, you have to keep asking
questions.

Five fast facts about asking questions:

1. The world's smartest people ask lots of
questions.

2. The man who doesn't ask questions doesn't
care or is afraid.

3. The man who is afraid to ask questions doesn't

know who to ask, is worried about sounding dumb, or is afraid of the answer.

4. The man who is afraid of the answer wants to believe something is true no matter what—even if it's not true—or is more afraid of the answerer's rebuke than of the answer itself.

5. Fortunately, God doesn't rebuke you when you ask honest questions.

a. Is it okay to ask questions when praying to God? (See Habakkuk 1:12–13.)
b. Is it okay to ask God, "Why did You let this happen?" (See Malachi 3:13–15.)
c. Is it okay to ask questions about God's Word? (See Acts 8:30–35.)
d. Is it okay to ask questions in church? (See Acts 15:1–11.)

Pray:

Yes, Lord, I want to say "Thank You!" for encouraging me to ask questions. That's helpful and motivating to me. I want to love You with all my heart, soul, strength, and mind.

Seeing the Really Big Picture
Read Luke 24:13–53

Key Verse:

*He said to them, "This is what I told you while I was
still with you: Everything must be fulfilled that
is written about me in the Law of Moses,
the Prophets and the Psalms."*
LUKE 24:44 NIV

Understand:

- *How well did Jesus (and later the disciples) know the Old Testament scriptures?*
- *How important is it for you to know the Bible cover to cover?*

Apply:

Once you see the big picture, you'll always be able to
see the Bible's design!

One Author, Forty Writers

Unlike other books, the Bible doesn't list any
author on the cover or title page. Then again, the
Bible isn't just any book! God is the Author. He
inspired a diverse group of forty individuals to write
the Bible over the course of sixteen hundred years.
The first writer was Moses, who penned the first
five books. Other important writers include David,

Solomon, Isaiah, Jeremiah, Ezekiel, Daniel, Hosea, Matthew, Mark, Luke, Paul, James, and Peter. The last writer was John, who wrote the fourth Gospel, three letters, and the book of Revelation. The Holy Spirit guided all of these individuals to write what they did.

Sixty-Six Books, One Story

The Bible contains a total of sixty-six books. Because God inspired all the writers, the Bible contains a unified message from beginning to end. In fact, the opening page talks about the beginning of time. The last page talks about the end of time as you know it. In between, the story of the Bible unfolds in all its drama, conflict, violence, irony, and glory. The Hero of the Bible is Jesus Christ. The enemies of Jesus Christ are Satan, evil people, and death. Everything and everybody in the first three-fourths of the Bible foreshadow the life, death, burial, and resurrection of Jesus Christ (or the ultimately futile opposition of His enemies).

There's more!

Pray:

Yes, Lord, I want to say "Thank You!" that I'm reading and studying the Bible. I want to keep doing it long after I finish this book.

Seeing More of the
Really Big Picture
Read Acts 6:1–7

Key Verse:

And the word of God continued to increase,
and the number of the disciples multiplied greatly
in Jerusalem, and a great many of the priests
became obedient to the faith.
ACTS 6:7 ESV

Understand:

- *How much of the Bible have you already read?*
- *How much would you like to read over the next ten or twelve months?*

Apply:

Over time, be sure you make it a goal to read all sixty-six books of the Bible. True, when you finish, you may think, *Wow, I didn't get all of that!* That's why it's great to make it a priority to read the whole Bible every year.

To do that, make it a practice to buy Barbour Publishing's bestselling *Daily Wisdom for Men* every autumn. Then use its "Read Thru the Bible in a Year Plan" in the back of every annual edition.

Once you see the really big picture, reading through the Bible makes a lot more sense.

One Work, Two Testaments

Like some books, the Bible is divided into two parts (called *testaments*, which is another word for *covenants*). The following lists clearly show how each testament is divided into four distinct, logical sections:

Old Testament

    1. Pentateuch: Genesis–Deuteronomy (five books written by Moses)

    2. History: Joshua–Esther (mostly anonymous authors)

    3. Literature: Job–Song of Songs (primarily by David and Solomon)

    4. Prophets: Isaiah–Malachi (by more than fifteen authors)

New Testament

    1. Gospels: Matthew–John (by four writers)

    2. Acts (by Luke)

    3. Letters: Romans–Jude (by Paul, James, Peter, John, and Jude)

    4. Revelation (by John)

Pray:

Yes, Lord, I want to say "Thank You!" for challenging me to read the entire Bible. You know what I have and haven't read so far. More great vistas and rewards ahead!

The Old Testament's
First Five Books
Read Genesis 15:1–6

Key Verse:

*And Abram believed the L*ORD*, and the L*ORD
counted him as righteous because of his faith.
GENESIS 15:6 NLT

Understand:

- *What does Moses have to teach us 3,500 years later?*
- *Who taught Moses?*

Apply:

Before you read the whole Bible, it's wise to look at each section of the Bible in more depth, starting with its first five books, also called the Pentateuch. Moses, one of the earliest and greatest prophets of God's people, wrote these books. God clearly chose Moses, called him to service, and revealed to him what to write in each of these five foundational books of the Bible.

Moses wrote these books in a straightforward, selective narrative format. (This means that he provides only selected narratives, not all the stories that could possibly be told about Adam and Eve, Noah,

Abraham, etc.) His narratives of creation are breathtaking. Moses went on to record important epic stories of early human history. Then he recorded the stories of God at work to create a nation that would be His witness to the world. Sadly, this nation (Israel) often turned from God, with disastrous results.

In these five books, Moses also included quite a bit of discourse (by God and Moses), several beautiful poetic sections (by God, Moses, and possibly Moses' sister Miriam), and a few important genealogical records (we'll see the value of those records later in scripture).

Expectations of a coming Messiah (Jesus Christ) appear throughout the books of Moses, from Genesis (3:15) to Deuteronomy (18:15).

Pray:

Yes, Lord, I want to say "Thank You!" for promising to bless the world through Abraham, the father of all who believe and trust in You.

The Old Testament's Next Twelve Books

Read Joshua 1:1–18

Key Verse:

"This Book of the Law shall not depart from your mouth, but you shall meditate on it day and night, so that you may be careful to do according to all that is written in it. For then you will make your way prosperous, and then you will have good success."

JOSHUA 1:8 ESV

Understand:

- *True or False? "Experience is the best teacher—especially the experiences of others who have gone before us."*
- *In Romans 15:4, what did Paul say about the value of the Hebrew scriptures?*

Apply:

Before you read the Old Testament, it's wise to look at the second section in more depth. That section is the history books, and it contains twelve books. Joshua, Ezra, and others wrote these books. They tell the story of God's people, the Israelite nation, for a thousand years from the death of Moses (around 1400 BC) until the completion of the Old Testament (after 450 BC). Like Moses did, Joshua, Ezra, and the other authors wrote these books in a straightforward, selective narrative format.

The narratives of Joshua's early exploits are riveting. Joshua then recorded how the Israelites divided up and settled the Promised Land. Sadly, the Israelites often rebelled against the Lord, fought against each other and—after a period of great prosperity—ultimately fought again and split into two kingdoms. The Northern Kingdom, Israel (ten Israelite tribes), never turned back to the Lord, and eventually the Assyrian Empire conquered it (722 BC). The Southern Kingdom, Judah (two tribes), turned back to the Lord on several occasions, but eventually the newly dominant Babylonian Empire conquered it (586 BC).

After the seventy years of Babylonian captivity, a remnant of the people from Judah (and Israel) returned to the former Promised Land, eventually rebuilt Jerusalem, and sought to start over. In these twelve books of history, you'll find not just narrative but also discourse, poetry, prayers, and genealogies.

Pray:

Yes, Lord, I want to say "Thank You!" for the way You challenged, strengthened, and blessed Joshua. Please do all three in my life as well.

The Old Testament's Second Half
Read Psalm 1:1–6

Key Verse:

*He is like a tree planted by streams of water that
yields its fruit in its season, and its leaf does
not wither. In all that he does, he prospers.*
PSALM 1:3 ESV

Understand:

- *God richly blesses the man who does
  what?*
- *Do you want to be a God-blessed man? If
  so, when?*

Apply:

The rest of the Hebrew scriptures offer a lot of variety in style, tone, and content. This second half of the Hebrew scriptures includes the two following sections:

Literature. This section contains five books. David and Solomon wrote most of them, but they also include writings by Moses and many other contributors. These five books present the best of five kinds of Hebrew literature written between 1450 BC (Psalm 90 by Moses, probably before the Lord called him to deliver the Israelites from slavery in

Egypt) and 450 BC (Psalm 137 by Jeremiah, according to ancient Jewish tradition). The types of literature include drama, worship lyrics, wise sayings, a sermon, and a love song.

The anticipation of the coming of Jesus Christ is especially evident in more than a dozen psalms that include detailed messianic prophecies.

Prophets. This section contains seventeen books, written by Isaiah, Jeremiah, Ezekiel, and Daniel (known as the *major prophets*) and twelve other prophets (known as the *minor prophets*—but "minor" only in the sense that they wrote shorter books). Isaiah and the others wrote these books in the prophetic genre, largely in poetic form with some narrative interludes. These books contain a series of messages from God dating from 850 BC to sometime after 450 BC.

Many of these prophetic messages call the Israelites to repent of their sins and turn back to the Lord. Other messages foretell future events, including God's coming judgment on the kingdoms of Israel and Judah and surrounding nations.

The expectation of the coming Messiah is also strongly apparent throughout these prophetic writings.

Pray:

Yes, Lord, I want to say "Thank You!" for promising to bless the man who meditates on Your Word day and night. I want to start by taking today's key verse to heart.

The Silent Years
Read Daniel 9:1–27

Key Verse:

"Know and understand this: From the time the word goes out to restore and rebuild Jerusalem until the Anointed One, the ruler, comes, there will be seven 'sevens,' and sixty-two 'sevens.'"

DANIEL 9:25 NIV

Understand:

- *If Jesus had been born fifty years earlier or fifty years later, would it have mattered? Why or why not?*
- *True or False? "In His wisdom, God orchestrated Christmas and Calvary at just the right time." If true, why does it matter?*

Apply:

After the close of the Old Testament, it appears that God was silent for more than four hundred years. Why did God wait so long before sending Jesus Christ to earth?

A prophecy in the book of Daniel holds part of the key to the answer. In Daniel 9:24–27, the prophet foretold that more than four hundred years must pass from the return from captivity until the Messiah would come and be "cut off." That time was drawing near when Jesus began His public ministry among a people longing for and anticipating the Messiah's coming.

The cultural and political situation in Palestine during the first century AD also explains God's purpose in waiting so long. Three different peoples had a tremendous influence on the times of the life of Jesus Christ and His newborn church.

1. The Greeks. The Greeks had ruled the world, and their culture influenced the Romans. The Greeks passed from the scene politically, but their language survived as the universal world language for many years. This was the language in which the New Testament was written. Greek culture, particularly philosophy, influenced much thinking in the first century AD.

There's more!

Pray:

Yes, Lord, I want to say "Thank You!" for Your sovereignty and providence. Your plan from all eternity has been unfolding exactly as You decreed.

More About the Silent Years
Read Malachi 3:1–18

Key Verse:

"Ever since the time of your ancestors you have turned away from my decrees and have not kept them. Return to me, and I will return to you," says the LORD Almighty. "But you ask, 'How are we to return?'"

MALACHI 3:7 NIV

Understand:

- *What does Paul say in Galatians 4:4 about God's timing for sending His Son?*
- *How did God orchestrate everything? Mostly using good angels or mostly using unbelieving men?*

Apply:

Two more peoples had a tremendous influence on the times of the life of Jesus Christ and His newborn church:

2. The Romans. Some sixty years before the birth of Jesus Christ, the Roman Empire (the last great world empire) arose. The Romans ruled all of the Mediterranean area and the rest of the known world at that time. The Caesars brought world peace under one government, which aided the early church as it began to spread from Palestine. Also, the vastly improved transportation systems the Romans developed gave the first missionaries the opportunity to carry the Gospel of Jesus Christ to new areas. It wasn't until after AD 60 that local persecution against Christians started engulfing the empire.

3. *The Jews.* The Jewish people had lived in Palestine for nearly fourteen hundred years. Then they found themselves under the yoke of Rome, and most found it unpleasant. The Jewish people's hope was deliverance from Roman domination. Sadly, Judaism had degenerated from a religion based on faith into a weighty compilation of human laws and traditions. The leadership and masses no longer worshiped God, and soon Jerusalem and Palestinian Judaism were destroyed (AD 70).

Into this world situation Jesus Christ came to redirect people (all people, Jewish and Gentile) back to God. The Lord waited until the right time!

Pray:

Yes, Lord, I want to say "Thank You!" for Your right and perfect timing. The ancient empires didn't know that You orchestrated their rise and fall. Your ways are so much higher than man's.

The New Testament's First Five Books
Read John 1:1–18

Key Verse:

For the law was given through Moses;
grace and truth came through Jesus Christ.
JOHN 1:17 ESV

Understand:

- *What does God want you to do as you read the four Gospels?*
- *What does He want you to do as you read Acts?*

Apply:

Before you read the New Testament, it's wise to look at each section in more depth. The first two sections are:

The Gospels. This section contains four books, written by Matthew, Mark, Luke, and John. These four men tell us about the significance of the divinity, birth, life, ministry, teachings, miracles, suffering, death, burial, resurrection, ascension, heavenly reign, and future return of Jesus Christ. Matthew and the others wrote these books in the gospel genre, mostly in narrative style with a number of sections of discourse, some poetic passages and prayers, and two genealogies.

The key period of time the Gospels cover stretches from about 6 BC to about AD 30, which represents the years Jesus lived here on earth. The expectation of the coming Messiah is realized—and the Lord offers the Good News (the Gospel) of salvation to everyone.

Acts. This section contains one book, written by Luke. It picks up the narrative at the end of Jesus's time here on earth, records the birth of the church, and shows how the church spread from Jerusalem and Judah to Samaria, and then to many regions throughout the Roman Empire, from about AD 30 to AD 61. The church's message is clear: believe in Jesus Christ, the Savior of the world. Some met that Good News with open arms—many others with much resistance. The theme of Jesus Christ as the Messiah is strongly emphasized in this book.

Pray:

Yes, Lord, I want to say "Thank You!" for the Gospels and Acts. It's incredible to read about Your Son and our Lord and Savior, Jesus Christ, and His work through the apostles and early church.

The New Testament's Second Half
Read Romans 1:1–17

Key Verse:

For I am not ashamed of this Good News about Christ. It is the power of God at work, saving everyone who believes—the Jew first and also the Gentile.
ROMANS 1:16 NLT

Understand:

- *Is it surprising to you that a lot of the New Testament is written to problem-filled churches?*
- *If that isn't surprising to you, why is that?*

Apply:

Before you read the New Testament, it's wise to look at the longest and shortest sections in more depth:

Letters. This section contains twenty-one books, written by Paul, James, Peter, John, and Jude. These twenty-one books present what the life, ministry, and message of the church should (and shouldn't) look like. Most of the books address problems in the early churches. Many sections, however, provide positive explanations of Christian teachings and practices. Paul and the other authors wrote these books in the epistle genre, mostly as discourse with some poetry and prayers. Most of these books were written between AD 45 and AD 70, but John may have written his several shorter letters after AD 85. The theme of Jesus Christ as Messiah is clearly proclaimed throughout these letters.

Revelation. This section contains one book, written by the apostle John about AD 95. John wrote this book in an apocalyptic manner, enfolding poetry and discourse in a narrative framework. In many ways, this book echoes the passion and some of the themes of the Old Testament prophets: turn from your sins, turn back to God, and get ready for the Lord's pending judgments on the whole earth.

Interestingly, the theme of Revelation isn't so much *how the world ends* but rather *how will your life end—with you staying true to the Lord or not?* The Lord Jesus Christ is clearly worshiped as God's Son, the Messiah, and the Savior of the world.

Pray:

Yes, Lord, I want to say "Thank You!" for the Good News about Jesus Christ. It's Your power at work, saving everyone who trusts You. I am one of Yours—I believe.

Still More Silent Years
Read Revelation 22:1–21

Key Verse:

Then the angel said to me, "Everything you have heard and seen is trustworthy and true."
REVELATION 22:6 NLT

Understand:

- *In 2 Peter 3:8, the apostle told us to not forget something. What are we not to forget?*
- *In Psalm 90:4, the prophet Moses said something similar. Why has this truth been so important to remember all throughout history?*

Apply:

After the close of the New Testament, it appears that God has been silent for almost 2,000 years. In reality, God has been speaking powerfully through the Bible's sixty-six books, which easily fill a thousand pages in most Bibles.

During the past two millennia, God has been using scripture to build His church around the world. Today more than 2.5 billion people call themselves Christians. Even in the remotest corners of the world, despite intense persecution, people of every nation, people, and tongue are starting to believe.

Part of the key to the expansion of the church has been the translation, publication, reading, and teaching of the Bible among thousands of groups. That expansion has accelerated at a phenomenal rate over the past two generations.

Bible reading and studying isn't a luxury. It's the way the Christian faith takes root in your heart and is shared with others.

Before you wrap up the last two dozen pages of this *5-Minute Bible Study for Men*, start making a mental list. Include two, three, or four Christian friends you'd like to invite to study this book with you. Yes, you'll be all set to go. Still, there's nothing better than taking a few friends along to see the vistas of scripture with you!

Pray:

Yes, Lord, I want to say "Thank You!" that You live outside and far beyond what I see and know and think of as reality. All that I see, hear, smell, taste, and feel will one day pass away. I can't wait to be with You, in Your presence, in the new heavens and new earth.

God Wants You to Ask!
Read Matthew 7:7–11

Key Verse:

"Ask, and it will be given to you; seek, and you will find; knock, and it will be opened to you."
MATTHEW 7:7 ESV

Understand:

- *How would you feel if you had actively and repeatedly encouraged a loved one to tell you whenever that person has a specific need, but he never does?*
- *How would you feel if a long-forgotten second cousin showed up unannounced, says he hears you've done well for yourself, and then tells you exactly what he wants from you?*

Apply:

With two weeks left, let's enjoy some of the most famous vistas in scripture. Today, we're going to look at one found in the picturesque Sermon on the Mount.

Throughout His three years of public ministry, Jesus modeled the substantive value of prayer. Not just prayer in the air, but prayer to God our Father.

And not just prayer for something good, but detailed and specific prayers.

What's the most specific prayer you have ever prayed? How earnest were your prayers? Did you know you absolutely *needed* the Lord, and the Lord alone, to come through?

Sometimes the poor have an advantage. They know exactly what they need and when they need it. And they know exactly how to respond when the Lord answers such prayers. Yes, they cheer and thank God with all their heart, soul, strength, and might.

If only we could capture a bit more of their deep trust and dependence on God's guidance, goodness, and outright miracles. It would do something wonderful. It would increase our love, faith, and trust in Jesus. Just as it did for the disciples nearly 2,000 years ago.

Pray:

Thank You, Lord, for Your providential work and for Your answers to my specific prayers, which increase my faith and trust in You. I'm so glad You want me to turn to You, always.

God Wants to Make You More Loving

Read 1 Corinthians 12:31–13:13

Key Verse:

But earnestly desire the higher gifts.
And I will show you a still more excellent way.
1 CORINTHIANS 12:31 ESV

Understand:

- *What if your closest friend or loved one suddenly became 25 percent more loving to you? How long do you think it would take before you figured it out?*
- *What if you could become 10 percent more loving to your closest friends and loved ones? What would it take to make that happen?*

Apply:

What's the longest period of time that you and your wife or closest loved one have been apart? A week? A month? A year? Several years? Career-dominated jobs abound in the military, firefighting, professional sports, and many other fields of endeavor.

It was no different for the Twelve. Jesus called Peter and Andrew, James and John, and each of the other apostles to follow Him—and didn't wait around for an answer. It was either instant yes or automatic no.

What was Jesus trying to teach them during those three years of life together? A lot! But mostly, He showed them what the marvelous, amazing mercy, grace, and love of God looks like in flesh and blood.

As we read the Gospels, we sometimes miss the elbows and fist pumps, laughter and ribbing, humor and sarcasm of Jesus. Sometimes we miss the bone-tiring walks, the leisurely meals, the beachside BBQs. Everything, *everything*, Jesus said and did was done a hundred percent in love.

Pray:

Lord, I can't spend most of my time today with You, but You already know that. Still, I want to walk in step with Your will. Please infuse my heart with more of Your love.

The Hairs on Your Head
Read Acts 27:9–37

Key Verse:

*"Please eat something now for your own good.
For not a hair of your heads will perish."*
ACTS 27:34 NLT

Understand:

- *When Paul added that last statement,
  what kind of promise was he making?*
- *Was Paul's phrase meant to be understood
  literally or metaphorically?*

Apply:

After surviving the shipwreck, none of Paul's shipmates double-checked to make sure he hadn't lost
any hair. Instead, they were deeply moved that his
God-ordained promise came true. Not a man was
lost!

To understand Paul's use of the phrase "Not a
hair of your heads will perish," it's helpful to see how
it was used in biblical times. The phrase, it turns out,
had a long history.

The use of this phrase as a biblical metaphor
dates back before 1000 BC and the start of the
united Israelite monarchy under Saul, David, and

Solomon. Metaphors included "safety" (1 Samuel 14:45, 2 Samuel 14:11, and 1 Kings 1:52) and "huge number" (Psalm 40:12 and 69:4, both attributed to David).

Centuries later, both during and after the Babylonian Captivity, use of this phrase became literal. Its literal meanings included "safety" (Daniel 3:27) and "extreme grief" (Ezra 9:3).

During His public ministry here on earth, Jesus used this phrase literally and as a metaphor. Its literal meanings included "humanly impossible" (Matthew 5:36) and "divinely known in exact detail" (Matthew 10:30 and Luke 12:7). Its metaphorical meaning included "safety" (Luke 21:18).

During his apostolic ministry, Paul used this phrase with the metaphorical meaning of "safety" (Acts 27:34). Again, not a man was lost!

Pray:

Yes, Lord, I want to say "Thank You!" that You kept Your promise to Paul and his shipmates. It reminds me to trust Your promises about forgiving my sins, giving me eternal life, and so much more.

What Should You Think About?
Read Philippians 4:8–13

Key Verse:

Whatever is true, whatever is noble, whatever is right, whatever is pure, whatever is lovely, whatever is admirable—if anything is excellent or praiseworthy—think about such things.
PHILIPPIANS 4:8 NIV

Understand:

- *How many minutes per day (outside of work) do you actively choose what you're going to think about?*
- *Do you tend to actively choose based on intentional plans or the spur of the moment?*

Apply:

One of men's greatest fears is someone figuring out what they think about. Yet, what you think about defines almost everything else about you. So why the deep fear? And how do you overcome it?

The apostle Paul provided the answer in the verse quoted above. The verse's eight terms describe the Lord and His Word and fill its pages from Genesis 1 to Revelation 22. As well, the eight terms describe a number of biblical heroes. Best of all? They can describe you too!

The biggest surprise? How many of the biblical heroes are *women*, both ideal and real. *Ideal* women like Wisdom and the Virtuous Woman. *Real* women like Ruth, Rebekah, Rachel, and many others. Yes, it's good to think about them (instead of ignore them, which we guys are prone to do).

The last of the eight terms—praiseworthy and its synonyms—describes Abel (Hebrews 11:4), Enoch (Hebrews 11:5), Job (Job 29:11), Paul and Silas (Acts 15:40), Phoebe (Romans 16:1), and local church elders (Titus 1:7). Like the other seven terms, it describes both someone's character and what he thinks about. Each day, may you be a praiseworthy thinker. A great way to do that is to start every day going through a couple more pages in this *5-Minute Bible Study for Men* of course!

Like Paul, you can actively choose to think about what is true, noble, right, pure, lovely, admirable, excellent, and praiseworthy. If so, what you say and do will eventually reveal your Christlike character to a watching world.

Pray:

Yes, Lord, I want to say "Thank You!" that You and Your Word can fill my thoughts with all that is true, noble, right, pure, lovely, admirable, excellent, and praiseworthy.

What You Can Learn
from a Biblical Woman
Read Mark 12:41–44

Key Verse:

*"They all gave out of their wealth; but she, out of her
poverty, put in everything—all she had to live on."*
MARK 12:44 NIV

Understand:

- *When you filled out your latest tax
  returns, were you surprised by how little
  or by how much charitable giving you
  had done this past year?*
- *Are you willing to consider heeding the
  poor widow's example?*

Apply:

The poor widow in today's reading walks into the
Women's Court in front of the Temple. You can
imagine her rehearsing God's promises—and what
she has prayerfully decided to do. As Jesus watches,
she stops in front of a funnel-shaped offering recep-
tacle. She reaches out her hand and drops in her last
two small bronze coins.

Jesus knew this widow well. Yes, it's true, He
knows all widows. And He knew this poor woman

had no property and no close family to take care of her. Therefore, since it was something He did often, it's likely that Jesus motioned for one of His disciples to follow after her and quietly give her several silver coins.

Still, think about this poor widow's example.

First, she showed that no gift is too large. Jesus said she put in more than all the other contributors. She put in all she had to live on. Now, of course, she could do this because she wasn't obligated to care for anyone else. Scripture teaches that your obligation to care for your family's real needs supersedes any gift you desire to give. Giving isn't a way to shirk our God-given responsibilities at home.

Second, this poor widow showed that no gift is too small. Her two small coins couldn't even buy the smallest bird to sacrifice or eat. How in the world could her miniscule donation make any difference? To Jesus, though, it made all the difference. That small donation proved that this poor widow was fully and wholly dedicated to the Lord her God. Her love, trust, and sheer bravery is moving. It clearly moved Jesus, who honored her here and in Luke 21:1–4.

Pray:

Yes, Lord, I want to say "Thank You!" for all of the Bible's heroes, both men and women. May I follow the poor widow's example in the ways I give in coming days and weeks.

The Apostles Wrote with the Old Testament in Mind
Read Philippians 2:5–11

Key Verse:

At the name of Jesus every knee should bow, in heaven and on earth and under the earth, and every tongue acknowledge that Jesus Christ is Lord, to the glory of God the Father.
PHILIPPIANS 2:10–11 NIV

Understand:

- *What does it mean that one day every knee will bow at the name of Jesus?*
- *What does it mean that every tongue will acknowledge that Jesus Christ is Lord?*

Apply:

God the Father has given Jesus Christ the greatest honor in the universe. One day, everyone "in heaven and on earth and under the earth" (Philippians 2:10 NIV) will do two things. First, "every knee [will] bow" (v. 10) in submission to Jesus Christ. Second, everyone will audibly "acknowledge that Jesus Christ is Lord, to the glory of God the Father" (v. 11).

These words take us back to 700 BC. In a majestic passage, Isaiah 45:18–24, the Lord (*Yahweh*) spoke to the nations. He described Himself as Creator of the heavens and earth (v. 18), as the One and only Lord God (vv. 18, 21, 22), as One who speaks only truth (vv. 19, 23), as the only One who knows the future (v. 21), and as "a righteous God and a Savior" (v. 21 NIV).

Then the Lord issued these words through the prophet Isaiah: "Turn to me and be saved, all you ends of the earth; for I am God, and there is no other. By myself I have sworn, my mouth has uttered in all integrity a word that will not be revoked: Before me every knee will bow; by me every tongue will swear" (vv. 22–23 NIV).

When Paul wrote to the Philippian believers, he was clearly applying this stirring prophecy to Jesus Christ. What's more, he was saying that Jesus is the Lord (*Yahweh*). (Paul wrote the book of Philippians in ancient Greek, which had no equivalent to "*Yahweh*." But we know he meant that Jesus is *Yahweh* because Isaiah explicitly used that name for God five times in the passage Paul references.)

In the end, the question isn't, "Is Jesus Lord?" He *is*, now and for eternity. Instead, the question is: "Have you acknowledged that fact in your own life?" How good it is to gladly acknowledge His place in the universe and in your life, here and now.

Pray:

Yes, Lord, I want to say "Thank You!" that the New Testament wasn't written divorced from the Old Testament. Instead, it proclaims the fruition of all that the prophets wrote.

What You Can Learn from the Virtuous Woman

Read Proverbs 31:10–31

Key Verse:

Who can find a virtuous and capable wife?
She is more precious than rubies.
PROVERBS 31:10 NLT

Understand:

- *Do the women in your life tend to enjoy or get annoyed at today's scripture passage?*
- *If you don't know, ask!*

Apply:

Only the Lord Himself knows how many women's articles, women's Bible studies, women's talks, and women's retreats have extolled the Virtuous Woman described in today's reading. The only problem is they usually ignore the fact that the entire book of Proverbs was written to *men*.

In other words, today's reading is a challenge to *men*. It's for you. That changes things up, doesn't it? But it's all good. This scripture passage explains four specific ways a good husband can encourage his wife to beautifully and actively flourish in every area of her life.

Cherishing. The good husband recognizes the true value of his wife as a person (31:10). He sees her as God's priceless, one-of-a-kind masterpiece. He knows her worth is far above precious jewels.

Supporting. The good husband believes in the potential of his wife (31:11). He doesn't put her in a box called home only to let her lie there dormant. Instead, he allows her to be productive and fulfilled both in and out of the home (31:16, 20).

Listening. The good husband realizes the importance of listening to (and learning from) the wisdom of his wife (31:26). He is spared from many rash and foolish actions when he respects her faithful love and wisdom.

Praising. The good husband praises the virtues and accomplishments of his wife (31:29). He doesn't flatter her but praises his wife for her fear of God (31:30) and her successful endeavors (31:31). He lets others know how much he cherishes her.

Pray:

*Yes, Lord, I want to say "Wow!" I don't know how
I missed this all these years. Okay, maybe I do.
May I cherish, support, listen to, and praise
the godly women in my life.*

What Time Is It, Abraham?
Read Genesis 15:1–21

Key Verse:

He took him outside and said, "Look up at the sky and count the stars—if indeed you can count them." Then he said to him, "So shall your offspring be." Abram believed the LORD, and he credited it to him as righteousness.
GENESIS 15:5–6 NIV

Understand:

- *Did you notice the word "count" appears twice in today's key verse? How does Abraham's way of counting differ from the Lord's way of counting?*
- *Did you notice the phrase "if you are able"(NKJV)? Ancient astronomers confidently said there were 1,056 stars. So, why did the Lord remark, "if you are able"?*

Apply:

So many questions come to mind when you carefully read and study today's scripture passage. One of the biggest questions: does this chapter cover one rather full day or two separate occasions? Literary and biblical scholars wisely and rightly contend that it was a single day. Then comes the showstopper question: when today's key verse took place, what time of day was it?

At first, the answer seems obvious. It's the middle of the night, right? Abraham was in his tent praying. The Lord spoke to Abram (as he was called at that point). The Lord reinforced His promise and took Abram outside. They were no longer in Abram's tent. Before the Lord further reinforced His promise, He instructed Abram to do something. All is well, it seems, until the Lord added that pesky phrase, "if you are able."

Why would the Lord say that? Well, why not? After all, verse 12 talks about the sun going down, and verse 17 talks about after the sun had set and darkness settled over everything. If this is the same day, how can it be the middle of the night in verse 5?

As we see in Genesis 18:1—and as we see throughout that region and across southern Europe, southern Asia, and Latin America—many people rest during the hottest part of the day. It turns out that's the best explanation for what time of day it was in verse 5. In other words, the Lord was saying, in effect: "Abram, I'm asking you to do something that you can't see now, but you'll be able to see it tonight, just like almost every other night."

Then the Lord added, "So shall your offspring be."

In response, Abram "believed the LORD."

Pray:

Yes, Lord, I want to say "Thank You!" for our spiritual father in the faith, Abraham. Thank You for creating such a dramatic picture of what faith is all about.

How Old Are You, Moses?

Read Psalm 90:1–17

Key Verse:

*Our days may come to seventy years,
or eighty, if our strength endures.*
PSALM 90:10 NIV

Understand:

- *It's clearly understood that Moses wrote
Genesis through Deuteronomy during
the latter part of his life. Deuteronomy
31:2 and 34:7 specifically say that Moses
finished writing his fifth book shortly
before he died at age 120.*
- *So how old do you think Moses was when
he wrote Psalm 90?*

Apply:

Using the internal historical and literary evidence within Genesis, Exodus, Leviticus, Numbers, and Deuteronomy, it's safe to say that Moses wrote all five books after age 80 (when God called him) and no later than age 120 (when he died).

So, it's often assumed that Moses wrote Psalm 90 during that same span of time (again, after God called him but before he died 40 years later). Using the internal evidence within Psalm 90, however, can we get a better idea how old Moses was? Thankfully, the answer is yes!

First, you want to notice the allusions Moses made in Psalm 90 to the basic facts about Creation and the Flood accounts and Israel's early history. With the word *our* (v. 1), Moses identified with his people. With the phrase "all generations" (v. 1), Moses hinted at the literary structure of Genesis. With his poetic references to Creation (v. 2), Moses foreshadowed Genesis 1–2. With the word *dust* (v. 3 NIV), Moses foreshadowed Genesis 2:7 and 3:19. With the phrase "thousand years" (v. 4), Moses foreshadowed Genesis 5:27. With the word *flood* (v. 5), Moses foreshadowed Genesis chapters 6 to 9.

Second, you want to ponder what Moses said in verse 13. With his pleading question, "how long will it be?" (v. 13 NIV), Moses foreshadowed Genesis 15:13 and Exodus 1, and implied that the Lord hadn't yet stepped in to free His people from their terrible bondage in Egypt. Then, in today's key verse, Moses directly suggested that he's somewhere near that stage of life.

Bottom line: Moses probably was about 80 years old when he wrote Psalm 90. Finally, his heart was ready. The Lord then appeared to Moses in the burning bush (Exodus 3–5) and the rest is history!

Pray:

Yes, Lord, I see that You're waiting for me to have a ready heart before You call me into a new stage of life, and possibly into my greatest purpose on earth.

When Did God's People Know "All Have Sinned"?

Read Romans 3:9–23

Key Verse:

For all have sinned and fall short of the glory of God.
ROMANS 3:23 NKJV

Understand:

- *What scriptures did Paul know forward and backward?*
- *How often did he draw on those scriptures in his New Testament letters?*

Apply:

It's natural for most Christian men to read the New Testament and think it's all fresh, new revelation inspired by God. It is! That is, unless you think "fresh new" means divorced from what God revealed in the Old Testament.

Today's Bible reading ends with one of Paul's most famous, most memorized, and most quoted verses. It's today's key verse for good reason! But is it a brand-new Christian teaching?

If your study Bible offers cross-references, you'll quickly see that Paul was echoing the truth found in the very first verse in today's scripture reading. In turn, that verse is a quotation from Psalm 14:1 and Psalm 53:1.

Furthermore, additional cross-references will take you to 1 Kings 8:46; 2 Chronicles 6:36; Psalm 143:2; Proverbs 20:9; Ecclesiastes 7:20; Micah 7:2; and Jeremiah 2:9, 5:1–9, and 6:28.

And, that doesn't count New Testament cross-references to James 3:2 (probably written before Romans) and 1 John 3:8 and 3:10 (likely written later).

So, did Paul coin the idea that all have sinned? Hardly!

The reality is that most New Testament Gospel truths are firmly embedded in Old Testament teachings and prophecies.

That's good news indeed!

Pray:

Yes, Lord, I want to say "Thank You!" that the apostles and early church fathers weren't trying to invent a new religion. Instead, Your Holy Spirit helped them understand the fulfillment of the Hebrew scriptures in Jesus Christ and His Gospel. I believe!

You Can Obey This Command!
Read Ephesians 6:10–18

Key Verse:

*Pray in the Spirit at all times and on every occasion.
Stay alert and be persistent in your prayers
for all believers everywhere.*
EPHESIANS 6:18 NLT

Understand:

- *Which of God's commands do you find easiest to obey? "Do not murder"? Any others?*
- *Which of God's commands do you find hardest to obey? "Do not covet"? Any others?*

Apply:

When it comes to commands, Paul really packed them into today's Bible reading. Seven of the nine verses are bold commands for you to obey. Most have to do with taking on the power and armor of God. Duly noted! The last one, however, has to do with prayer. It's a doubleheader found in today's key verse.

The first half of the verse says, "Pray in the Spirit at all times and on every occasion." In other words, Paul wanted Christian men to confess their sins and ask to be filled with the Holy Spirit. That way, you can pray with a clean, filled, and bold heart—with the Holy Spirit leading and guiding you.

The second half of the verse says, "Stay alert and be persistent in your prayers for all believers everywhere." The first eight words make sense. The last four words make many guys cringe. They think, *How in the world would it be possible to do that even once?*

In Paul's day, he did it by cities and regions.

In our day, it's done by nations and continents.

How? See below.

Pray:

Yes, Lord, I want to say "Thank You!" for commanding Christian men to pray "for all believers everywhere." I want to do that very thing right now. Lord, I pray for Your protection and for the spiritual growth, endurance, maturity, and love of Christians in Muslim, Hindu, and Buddhist nations, and in other countries where Christians are at risk.

Why Are R-Rated Stories in the Bible?

Read Judges 19:16–30

Key Verse:

*He said, "Get up! Let's go!" But there was no answer.
So he put her body on his donkey and took her home.
When he got home, he took a knife and cut his
concubine's body into twelve pieces. Then he sent one
piece to each tribe throughout all the territory of Israel.*
JUDGES 19:28–29 NLT

Understand:

- *Does the Bible usually whitewash or san-
  itize the stories it tells? Why or why not?*
- *Does the Bible usually tell us the moral of
  the story? Why or why not?*

Apply:

The first seven books of the Bible all contain stories
that make good men wince. Murder. Rape. Slaughter.
Incest. Pillaging. Prostitution. Annihilation. Gang
rape. The short book of Ruth is the first Bible book
that's only PG-13. Then it's back to more sex and
violence at every turn from 1 Samuel to 2 Chronicles. The next two short books dial it back to PG-13,
but Esther...well, you get the idea. Sex and violence

and more sex and violence.

One of the Bible's most disturbing stories is found in today's reading. The book of Judges repeatedly shocks, and the appendices drive home the utter terror of these bookends: "In those days Israel had no king; all the people did whatever seemed right in their own eyes" (Judges 17:6 and 21:25 NLT).

In this case, the ancient moral of the story is obvious. The contemporary moral is no less terrifying: if you do whatever seems right in your own eyes, there is no limit to how depraved you can be.

In a world hell-bent on the opiates of pick-and-choose reality, you have to fight hard to stay grounded in God and His Word.

If you let down your guard. . .if you forget that bad company corrupts good morals. . .if you give in to the world's blatant lies. . .if you shake your fist at God and decide to do whatever you want. . .your own life story soon will be R-rated.

Week in and week out, you see the tragic stories of other men played out in real life. In their wake? Sex and violence and broken lives and God's judgment.

Why is the Bible so honest? For very good reasons indeed.

Pray:

Yes, Lord, I didn't enjoy today's Bible study. Maybe that was the point. I've already let down my guard. I repent. I turn from the errors of my way. I turn back to You. Cleanse me, fill me, and lead me in Your paths, I pray.

Why Does Mark 16
Have Alternate Endings?

Read Mark 16:1–20

Key Verse:

*Trembling and bewildered, the women went out
and fled from the tomb. They said nothing
to anyone, because they were afraid.*

MARK 16:8 NIV

Understand:

- *If today's key verse were the last verse in
  Mark's Gospel, why might Mark have
  stopped right in the middle of the action?*
- *Why else might Mark have stopped so
  abruptly in the middle of the resurrection
  story?*

Apply:

Virtually all modern English Bible translations
include notes within the text itself and in footnotes
indicating uncertainties about the last chapter in
Mark's Gospel.

What is certain is that Mark 16 ends abruptly at
today's key verse in the two oldest extant codices of
the New Testament.

The first, *Codex Vaticanus*, includes small symbols

to indicate where the scribes knew that variants existed in some of the biblical manuscripts within their scriptorium's library. These match up with what Greek New Testament scholars know today, even though the meaning of the small symbols weren't deciphered until 1995.

In that first codex, however, no small symbols appear at Mark 16:8. Instead, the scribes left near half of that particular page blank. That happens nowhere else. They wanted to leave no uncertainty about the fact that ancient manuscripts included alternate endings, and many included what we call Mark 16:9–20.

We have good reasons to believe that from the get-go, multiple copies of some New Testament books were sent to a variety of churches throughout a given region of the Roman Empire. It's very possible that Mark did the same. It's also possible that the Holy Spirit inspired Mark to create versions with alternate endings.

If Mark intentionally ended some manuscripts at today's key verse, he likely hoped that Christians would read them to their households, provoking not-yet-Christians to ask, "What? Why does he end the story so abruptly? What happened?"

Pray:

Yes, Lord, I want to say "Thank You!" for preserving the scriptures down through the ages. Before now, I didn't realize the abrupt ending of Mark might have been intentional. Please keep using this Gospel to win millions more to faith.

Why Is Ecclesiastes in the Bible?
Read Ecclesiastes 1:1–18

Key Verse:

The words of the Teacher, son of David, king in Jerusalem: "Meaningless! Meaningless!" says the Teacher. "Utterly meaningless! Everything is meaningless."
ECCLESIASTES 1:1–2 NIV

Understand:

- *Have you read all twelve chapters of Ecclesiastes at some point in the past?*
- *If so, what did you think of this one-of-a-kind book?*

Apply:

This fourth book of Hebrew literature explores a nagging age-old question: what is the meaning of life? This poetic essay or sermon, probably written by Solomon about halfway through his reign as king of Israel, ponders the *apparent* meaninglessness of life "under the sun."

The phrase "under the sun" aptly describes Solomon's earth-bound perspective through this book. He wasn't looking at life as the Lord in heaven sees it, but from the perspective of an immensely wise, fabulously wealthy, and politically powerful individual here on earth. From his famed vantage point, Solomon bookended Ecclesiastes by saying, "Everything is meaningless" (1:2 and 12:8 NIV).

Nevertheless, throughout this book Solomon alludes to basic beliefs in God's justice, graciousness, sovereignty, omniscience, transcendence, revelation, mystery, creative power, and eternal nature. Solomon wrapped up the book by saying: "Here is the conclusion of the matter: Fear God and keep his commandments, for this is the duty of all mankind. For God will bring every deed into judgment, including every hidden thing, whether it is good or evil" (12:13–14 NIV).

Solomon left it up to the reader to decide who God is (the Lord?) and how He reveals His commands (scripture?). It's quite likely that Solomon simply assumed his readers already were well versed in the commands the Lord God in heaven had revealed to Moses and other prophets.

It's also possible that Solomon may have distributed copies of this book to foreign visitors as a means of provoking their interest in the God of Israel.

Pray:

Yes, Lord, I want to say "Thank You!" for the book of Ecclesiastes. I'm still not quite sure what to make of it. Then again, this might be a good book to read with one of my more philosophical and not-yet-Christian friends.

Present or Future Tense
Read Malachi 1:11–14

Key Verse:

"But my name is honored by people of other nations from morning till night. All around the world they offer sweet incense and pure offerings in honor of my name. For my name is great among the nations,"
says the Lord *of Heaven's Armies.*
Malachi 1:11 nlt

Understand:

- *In a footnote for today's key verse, the* nlt *translators say they used present tense but the prophet's meaning may have been future tense.*
- *In a footnote for this same verse, the* esv *translators say they used future tense but the prophet's meaning may have been present tense.*

Apply:

Present or future tense? "Is" or "will be"? In exploring this small but important question, it's helpful to consider the following historical events described in great detail in God's Word:

- Sometime near 600 BC, Nebuchadnezzar issued a public statement of praise to the Most High, the King of heaven (Daniel 4:34–37). This statement was well-known in Babylonia, but it also reached many other cities throughout his empire.
- In 538 BC, King Cyrus of Persia issued a statement in praise of the Lord, the God of heaven, throughout his kingdom (2 Chronicles 36:22–23 and Ezra 1:1–4).
- Sometime near 535 BC, Darius the Mede sent a statement of praise to the God of Daniel to the people throughout the known world, which comprised at least 120 provinces (Daniel 6:25–27).

This makes at least two worldwide statements of praise to God within ninety years of the writing of the book of Malachi, which many scholars believe was written close to 445 BC. That same year, King Artaxerxes issued letters to the governors of the regions west of the Euphrates River in support of Nehemiah's mission to rebuild Jerusalem (Nehemiah 2:7–9).

In Malachi's day, therefore, it's likely that the Lord's name truly "is" great and feared among the nations!

Pray:

Yes, Lord, I want to say "Thank You!" that Your great name has been feared all throughout history. Amen!

Devotional Inspiration for Every Man!

3-Minute Prayers for Men
This devotional prayer title packs a powerful dose of inspiration into just-right-sized readings for men of all ages and backgrounds. Each of these 180 prayers, written specifically for devotional quiet time, meets you right where you are—and is complemented by a relevant scripture and question for further thought.

Paperback / 978-1-64352-043-8 / $4.99

3-Minute Devotions for Men
Written especially for the modern man, this devotional packs a powerful dose of challenge and encouragement into just-right-sized readings for men of all ages. Minute 1: scripture to meditate on; Minute 2: a short devotional reading; Minute 3: a prayer to jump-start a conversation with God.

Paperback / 978-1-68322-250-7 / $4.99

You're reading the
WRONG WAY

◇◇◇◇◇◇◇◇◇◇◇◇◇◇◇◇◇◇◇◇◇◇◇◇◇

MAGI reads from right to left, starting in
the upper-right corner. Japanese is read
from **right** to **left**, meaning that action,
sound effects, and word-balloon order are
completely reversed from English order.

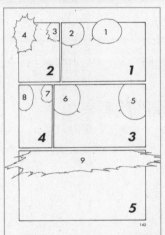

Dr.STONE

STORY BY
RIICHIRO INAGAKI

ART BY
BOICHI

One fateful day, all of humanity turned to stone. Many miller
later, Taiju frees himself from petrification and finds him
surrounded by statues. The situation looks grim—until he r
into his science-loving friend Senku! Together they plan to res
civilization with the power of science!

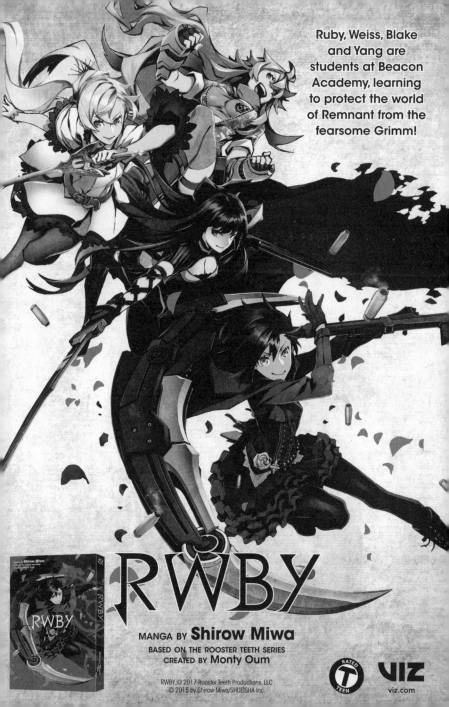

DEMON SLAYER
KIMETSU NO YAIBA

Story and Art by
KOYOHARU GOTOUGE

In Taisho-era Japan, kindhearted Tanjiro Kamado makes a living selling charcoal. But his peaceful life is shattered when a demon slaughters his entire family. His little sister Nezuko is the only survivor, but she has been transformed into a demon herself! Tanjiro sets out on a dangerous journey to find a way to return his sister to normal and destroy the demon who ruined his life.

Black✦Clover

STORY & ART BY YUKI TABATA

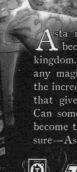

Asta is a young boy who dreams of becoming the greatest mage in the kingdom. Only one problem—he can't use any magic! Luckily for Asta, he receives the incredibly rare five-leaf clover grimoire that gives him the power of anti-magic. Can someone who can't use magic really become the Wizard King? One thing's for sure—Asta will never give up!

www.viz.com

Kidnapped by the Demon King and imprisoned in his castle, Princess Syalis is...bored.

Sleepy Princess in the Demon Castle

Story & Art by
KAGIJI KUMANOMATA

Captured princess Syalis decides to while away her hours in the Demon Castle by sleeping, but getting a good night's rest turns out to be a lot of work! She begins by fashioning a DIY pillow out of the fur of her Teddy Demon guards and an "air mattress" from the magical Shield of the Wind. Things go from bad to worse—for her captors—when some of Princess Syalis's schemes end in her untimely— if temporary—demise and she chooses the Forbidden Grimoire for her bedtime reading...

VIZ

MAGI

Volume 35
Shonen Sunday Edition

Story and Art by
SHINOBU OHTAKA

MAGI Vol.35
by Shinobu OHTAKA
© 2009 Shinobu OHTAKA
All rights reserved.
Original Japanese edition published by SHOGAKUKAN.
English translation rights in the United States of America, Canada, the United Kingdom,
Ireland, Australia and New Zealand arranged with SHOGAKUKAN.

*ORIGINAL COVER DESIGN / Yasuo SHIMURA+Bay Bridge Studio

Translation & English Adaptation ◇ John Werry

Touch-up Art & Lettering ◇ Stephen Dutro

Editor ◇ Mike Montesa

Printed in Canada

Published by VIZ Media, LLC
P.O. Box 77010
San Francisco, CA 94107

10 9 8 7 6 5 4 3 2 1
First printing, April 2019

viz.com

SHINOBU OHTAKA

*King's Vessel Users—
Battles Without Honor
or Humanity*

The End. ♡

MAGI
The labyrinth of magic
35

Staff

■ **Story & Art**

Shinobu Ohtaka

■ **Regular Assistants**

Hiro Maizima

Yuiko Akiyama

Megi

Aya Umoto

Mami Yoshida

Chidori Ishigo

■ **Editors**

Kazuaki Ishibashi

Makoto Ishiwata

Katsumasa Ogura

■ **Sales & Promotion**

Tsunato Imamoto

Yuta Uchiyama

■ **Designer**

Hajime Tokushige + Bay Bridge Studio

WHAT A *MESS!*

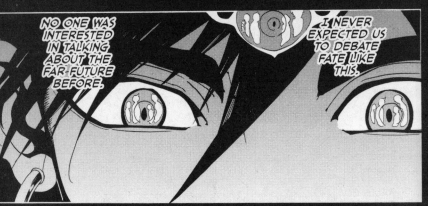

NO ONE WAS INTERESTED IN TALKING ABOUT THE FAR-FUTURE BEFORE.

I NEVER EXPECTED US TO DEBATE FATE LIKE THIS.

THIS IS GETTING NOWHERE! I SHOULD JUST DESTROY EVERYONE BUT *HIM!*

I SEE YOUR POINT.

HUH ?!

POOR IL-IRRAH!

BUT ....!!

SEIZING FATE MEANS DEFEATING OPPONENTS, RIGHT? THAT'S FINE FOR US, BUT WHAT ABOUT OTHER WORLDS?!

WHAT SHOULD WE DO?! HELP, SOLOMON!

...

...

SH- SHE'S STUB- BORN!

I REFUSE TO AGREE!! AFTER YOU STEAL ANOTHER GOD'S POWER, YOU'LL REMAKE THAT WORLD AND THE NEXT ONE AND ON AND ON! THAT'S JUST LIKE SOLOMON! I WILL FIGHT THAT TO THE BITTER END!

NO, EACH WORLD MUST BE FREE!! WE MUST FORTIFY THE WALLS TO PROTECT OURSELVES!

WE MUST SEIZE CONTROL OF FATE!! AND TEAR DOWN THE WALLS ABOVE US!

...

ONE LEVEL PAST IL-IRRAH? OR HIGHER? THAT FIGHT WOULD GO ON *FOREVER!*

BUT HOW FAR DO WE GO?

YOU ACT LIKE *HE* IS JUST AN ENERGY MASS, BUT I HEARD HIS *VOICE!* HE HAS A WILL JUST LIKE US!!

THAT'S RIGHT! IT IS ARRO-GANT!

...AND THEREBY SEIZE HOLD OF OUR FATE!

THE GODS OF HIGHER WORLDS HAVE THE POWER TO REORDER FATE IN LOWER WORLDS. THUS, I AGREE WITH ALIBABA AND SINBAD. WE SHOULD DESTROY THE VERTICAL BARRIERS...

NO, IL-IRRAH ISN'T LIKE US.

SOLOMON AND I USED ALL OF IL-IRRAH'S MAGOI MERELY TO ATTAIN ONE OTHER DIMENSION

GWOoo

...REQUIRES TAKING THE WHOLE WORLD THAT SOLOMON CREATED AND RETURNING IT TO RUKH!!!

SPIN SPIN

I SPENT FOREVER PONDERING THE USE OF MAGIC TO CONNECT DIMENSIONS! BUT IT TAKES THE POWER OF A GOD!! CONNECTING DIMENSIONS AGAIN...

BUT, UGO...

SILENCE

...

4 L P

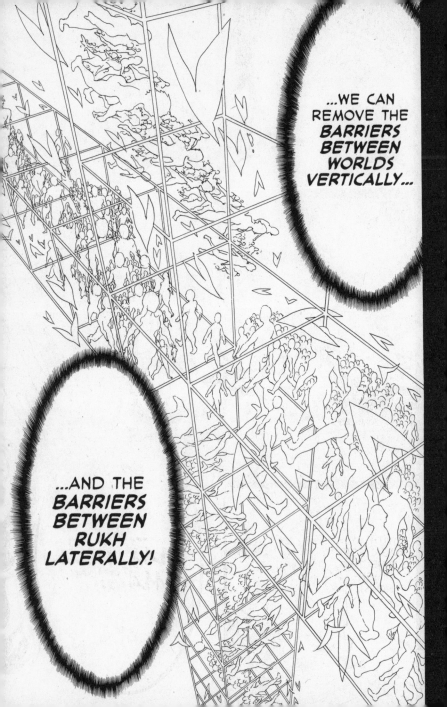

SO IT'S POSSIBLE TO UNIFY IL-IRRAH'S DIMENSION AND THIS WORLD!

YEAH! MAGIC CAN MOMENTARILY CONNECT DIMENSIONS!

HMM...

CONSIDER THE TALL BUILDINGS IN PARTEBIA.

SINBAD WANTS TO BREAK INTO HIGHER FLOORS AND DEFEAT THE GODS THERE.

THAT'S RIGHT.

IT'S LIKE WE'RE ON THE FIRST FLOOR.

WHICH IS BAD! PEOPLE HAVE THINGS THEY WANT TO DO!

God A

God B

God C

HE WANTS TO BREAK THE CEILINGS TO HIGHER WORLDS.

BUT TO DO THAT EVERYONE HAS TO DIE AND BECOME RUKH.

AND ALADDIN'S PLAN...

...CONNECTS EVERYONE LATERALLY.

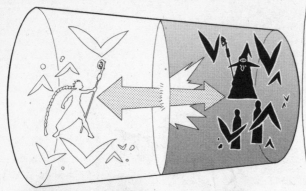

HE WANTS TO BREAK THE SACRED PALACE DIVIDING BLACK AND WHITE RUKH. BUT THEN A GOD WILL STILL CONTROL FATE.

SO WHAT DO WE DO?

RIGHT. CALM YOURSELF AND THINK THIS OVER!

I INTENDED TO ABANDON MY GREAT CAUSE UPON ENTERING THE SACRED PALACE, BUT I STILL CAN'T FORGET THOSE I ONCE LOVED, SO I REMAIN MERELY HUMAN.

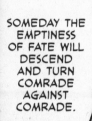

SOMEDAY THE EMPTINESS OF FATE WILL DESCEND AND TURN COMRADE AGAINST COMRADE.

THEN WHAT DO *YOU* SUGGEST? ARE YOU FINE WITH THE WORLD THAT KING SOLOMON CREATED?

WOULD YOU SIMPLY *IGNORE* THAT POSSIBILITY?

HOW COULD SHEBA HAVE

HEH...I SEE YOUR POINT.

...

"...AND COMMIT UNSPEAK-ABLE CRIMES!"

"PEOPLE FORMULATE DREAMS AND ACHIEVE THEM AND THEN WIELD WEAPONS TO PRESERVE THEM..."

THAT'S WHAT YOU'VE BECOME! HAVEN'T YOU NOTICED?!

BUT WE... YOU'LL DO ANYTHING TO PROTECT OTHERS!

IN THIS STRUGGLE, HAVE YOU LOST SIGHT OF YOURSELF?

?

IT'S ONLY NATURAL TO PROTECT YOUR FAMILY. ISN'T IT IRONIC HOW THOSE FEELINGS LEAD TO WAR?

FATHERS DEFEND THEIR FAMILIES, AND MOTHERS PRESERVE EMPIRES!

THEY GREW TOO ATTACHED TO OUR ACCOMPLISH- MENTS.

THAT'S JUST HOW OUR SPECIES IS!

BUT HUMAN BEINGS CANNOT WITHSTAND THAT OVER- WHELMING EMPTY FEELING!! AND YOU SAW HOW THAT ENDED!!!

THEY TRIED FIGHTING TO PROTECT THEIR FAMILIES, BUT IT WAS FUTILE! THEY WERE IN THE PALM OF SOMEONE'S HAND! THEY WERE PUPPETS OF A GOD! AND THAT'S FATE!

NO, WE WILL NOT ALLOW...

...FATE TO EXIST THIS WAY!!!!

SIM CAN ACC TI FA

EMPTINESS CAN EVEN CRUSH A GOD! UGO DEVOTED HIMSELF TO PRESERVING THE SAME WORLD ORDER, AND IT BROKE HIM! BUT I WON'T FALL INTO THAT RUT!

THE MAGICIANS DENIED FATE, LAUNCHING A WAR THAT DESTROYED THE WORLD!!

THEN ALLOW ME TO EXPLAIN! THIS FIGHT IS TO FREE EVERYONE FROM FATE!

IL-IRRAH WAS ABOVE US, BUT THERE'S ANOTHER GOD ABOVE IL-IRRAH!

SO YOU'RE DOING THIS TO FREE EVERYONE FROM FATE?

UGO USED MAGIC TO DEPOSE IL-IRRAH, BUT A MUCH GREATER POWER IS NECESSARY FOR OVERTURNING THE WHOLE ORDER!

THE GODS' EVERY WHIM CAN ALTER OUR FUTURE!

Night 347:
The Empty Feeling

...SINBAD'S CERTAINTIES *PARTIALLY* CAME TRUE?!

DOES THAT MEAN...

HM?

I ASK YOU!

HUH?!

No Breaking the rules!

SINBAD! ENOUGH OF THIS! THE SUN IS SETTING, SO THERE'S NO TIME!!

CLOMP

MANY PEOPLE FROM SINDRIA BECAME FALLEN, AND I ABSORBED THEIR BLACK RUKH.

THE PARTEBIAN EMPIRE INVADED AND DESTROYED THE FIRST KINGDOM OF SINDRIA.

ALIBABA, I'VE TOLD YOU THAT BEFORE.

THAT'S WHEN I STARTED HEARING DAVID'S VOICE.

THAT'S WHAT DAVID MEANT ABOUT CONTACTING A HALF-FALLEN SINGULARITY.

YES, I REMEMBER.

SILE

BEFORE I ESTABLISHED SINDRIA 'S CUP

...AND UR INK LED.

...BA!

Night 346:
A New Path Into the Future

...AND NOT SEEK ANYTHING FROM ANYONE ELSE!

I'VE DECIDED TO LIVE BY MY OWN WILL...

WHAT A WEIRDO! HE BELIEVED HE COULD GO BACK, JUST LIKE *YOU-KNOW-WHO!*

HE MADE THINGS FUN FOR A WHILE!

RMM

RMM

RMM

GOOD-BYE, ALIBABA

WOO HOO

HA HA... NO WAY!

CONNECT RUKH? WHAT DO YOU MEAN?

THIS MAGIC WILL CONNECT DIMENSIONS. CAN IT ALSO CONNECT *RUKH?*

YOU GUYS ARE INSIDE IL-IRRAH, AND AL-THAMEN IS SOMEWHERE ELSE.

WHEN PEOPLE IN MY WORLD DIE, THEY TURN INTO WHITE RUKH AND JOIN THE GREAT FLOW. BUT FALLEN PEOPLE TURN INTO BLACK RUKH AND REMAIN APART.

WHY DO PEOPLE SCATTER AFTER THEY DIE? ISN'T THERE SOME WAY TO CONNECT THEM ALL?

ALIBABA, WHEN YOU GO BACK, YOU'LL LEAVE US.

WHAT'S THAT STATUE? IT LOOKS COOL!

YOU'LL NEED A BODY WHEN YOU GO BACK, SO WE'RE MAKING ONE WITH THE ROCKS. AFTER ALL, WE'VE GOT LOTS OF TIME!

THAT'S WHEN YOU MUST PASS OVER.

LISTEN, ALIBABA. THIS MAXIMUM MAGIC WILL CONNECT DIFFERENT DIMENSIONS FOR ONLY A BRIEF MOMENT.

WILL I BE ABLE TO COME BACK HERE?

...

I WISH I COULD SEE HER...

HM? WHAT'S WRONG?

MY MOTHER...

HOW COME I FORGOT THIS FEELING?

GRIN

I WANNA SEE MY MOM!

HOW DO YOU COMMAND RUKH INSIDE ROCKS?! I'M NOT A MAGICIAN! CAN I EVEN DO THIS?!

IF YOU CAN'T USE THE MAGIC THEY DESIGN, THEN YOU'LL NEVER MAKE IT BACK!

OH...

LOTS OF PEOPLE! THEY HELPED ME, AND NOW THEY'RE IN TROUBLE!

ALI-BABA, WHO DO YOU WANNA MEET?

OH! THANKS, TESS!

I'LL TEACH YOU!

CUZ I'M BORED!

TPTPTP

HMM ...

YES.

WHEN YOU DIED, YOUR MOTHER WAS SAD.

MY MOTHER ISN'T ALIVE ANY-MORE.

OH, THAT'S TOO BAD.

WHAT ABOUT YOUR MOM?

TESS, THAT ISN'T YOUR DAD'S FORTE. HE ALWAYS LEFT THE BRAIN WORK TO UGO AND ME.

SMILE

YOU WORK HARD AT IT!

WON'T RETURNING ALIBABA TO LIFE REQUIRE SPIRIT INDUCTION?

NO, STRENGTH MAGIC. FIRST, HE MUST BREAK FREE OF THIS DIMENSION, SO...

HA HA HA

SHUT UP! I CAN MAKE MAGIC TOO! BRING ME SOMETHING TO WRITE WITH! I'LL DASH OFF A MAGICAL FORMULA IN NO TIME!

CHATTER

CHATTER

CHATTER

PLEASE! YOU GOTTA HELP ME!

AND I'VE NEVER HAD A GIRL-FRIEND!

WAHAHA

Y-YOU'VE NEVER MADE IT WITH A GIRL?! YOU POOR SOUL!

WELL, YOU... UM...

HUH ?!

DAD, HOW DO YOU MAKE MAGIC?

BUT, THEY'RE FROM ALIBABA'S WORLD, SO MAYBE HE CAN!

FIRST, WE SHOULD DEVISE MAGIC FOR SENDING HIM BACK!

THIS MATERIAL AND THESE WHITE RUKH AREN'T FROM ALMA TRAN, SO WE MAY NOT BE ABLE TO USE THEM.

...SO I'M FINE STACKING ROCKS RIGHT HERE!

WHY DO YOU WANT TO LIVE? I DON'T WANNA DO ANYTHING...

I WANT TO DO *LOTS* OF THINGS!

YEAH, GOOD QUESTION!

TESS...

I WANT TO SEE PEOPLE, PROTECT MY COUNTRY, KEEP PROMISES, ACHIEVE GOALS, AND LEARN NEW THINGS!

THIS IS AN INCREDIBLE FIND! RUKH ARE THE SOURCE OF MAGOI!!

WHOA!

YES?

UM, I'VE GOT A QUESTION!

What's up?

...

BECAUSE WE NEVER WANTED TO DO ANYTHING!

WE NEVER THOUGHT OF THAT!

CHATTER

CHATTER

EVERYONE HERE IS A PHANTOM. EVEN OUR BODIES. THERE'S NO RUKH, SO THERE'S NO MAGOI, SO WE CAN'T USE MAGIC.

OH, BUT THERE'S RUKH IN THESE ROCKS.

HUH?! THE *ROCKS*?!

NOPE.

AND THERE'S NO MAGOI IN *ME*?

THEY AREN'T PHANTOMS. THEY CAME FROM THE DIMENSIONAL RIFT.

DIMEN-SIONAL RIFT?

THAT BOY IS STRANGE.

I DON'T KNOW WHAT IT'S LIKE TO WANT TO LIVE.

HEY! YOU'RE MAGICIANS, SO HELP ME OUT HERE!

STARE

WE CAN'T. WE CAN'T USE MAGIC HERE.

HUH? WHY NOT?

I WANT TO RETURN TO LIFE!

THAT AGAIN?! JUST KEEP STACKING ROCKS! THEN MAYBE THINGS'LL WORK OUT!

NO, I HIGHLY DOUBT THAT!

Night 345:
Connecting Magics

ALIBABA IS STILL GOING AROUND QUESTIONING EVERYONE.

WHAT'S IT FEEL LIKE TO WANNA LIVE?

HEY, SETTA?

HMM...

I DON'T KNOW. BUT YOU WERE ALIVE ONCE.

THAT'S AWFUL!! I HAVE TO STOP HIM!

FOR HIM, SLAUGHTER IS JUST A MEANS OF REACHING LARGER GOALS. HE'S COLD-HEARTED AND DOESN'T CARE ABOUT FRIENDS OR FAMILY.

SORRY. YOU HAVE NO CHOICE BUT TO GROW EMOTIONLESS AS YOU ARE STUCK HERE WITH YOUR MEMORIES FOR ETERNITY.

NOT GONNA HAPPEN! YOU CAN'T LEAVE THIS DIMENSION!

KLAK KLAK KLAK

Fwk

BUT...

WHAT HAPPENS IF HE DOES THAT?

EXACTLY WHAT HE SAID.

DAVID SAID HE COULD RETURN TO LIFE IF HE BECAME ONE WITH SINBAD. WHAT DID HE MEAN?

POS-SESS?

HE'LL POSSESS SINBAD.

THEN HE'LL DESTROY YOUR WORLD JUST LIKE ALMA TRAN.

DESTROY MY WORLD?!!

WHEN DAVID
IS CERTAIN OF
SOMETHING,
IT BECOMES
TRUE. HE IS A
MANIFESTATION
OF FATE ITSELF!

HM? WAIT
A SECOND.

HE'S SOMEONE SPECIAL WHO WAS BORN WITH A GREAT MISSION IN LIFE.

AFTER ALL, *WE* GAVE UP ON LIFE AS SOON AS WE GOT HERE.

HE WAS THE ONLY PERSON HERE WHO WAS SURE THAT HE COULD RETURN TO LIFE. HIS SPIRITUAL FORTITUDE IS ASTOUNDING.

HE IS TRULY *FRIGHTEN-ING.*

DAVID...

HE HAD ALWAYS BEEN EVIL, BUT I TOOK HIM FOR A MERE RABBLE-ROUSER OR FANATIC.

I FELT A CHILL.

DIFFER-ENT?

HE'S DIFFERENT FROM US.

I WAS WRONG. WHEN HE IS CERTAIN OF SOMETHING, IT BECOMES TRUE.

HE WAS CRAZY. OR SO WE THOUGHT. BUT THEN SOMETHING AMAZING HAPPENED.

EVERYTHING HE HAD PREDICTED CAME TRUE.

THE GROUND SHOOK, A DIMENSIONAL RIFT FORMED, AND DAVID RETURNED TO THE EARTH.

THE KEY IS SOLOMON'S WISDOM. I CAN BECOME A GOD!

NOW I'LL SEIZE THE POWER OF THE SACRED PALACE!

H-HE'S...

DAVID KILLED OUR FRIENDS AND FAMILY, SO WE DESPISED HIM.

WE LET GO OF OUR ANGER AND SORROW AND ATTACHMENT TO LIFE BECAUSE TIME IS INFINITE.

BUT THEN WE FORGOT OUR EMOTIONS HERE.

WA HA HA!! JUST AS I EXPECTED! I FINALLY MADE CONTACT WITH A HALF-FALLEN SINGULARITY!!

BUT DAVID WAS DIFFERENT. HE WAS ELATED AND SPOKE OF BEING SURE ABOUT SOMETHING.

THE BOREDOM HERE HAS DRIVEN HIM BONKERS!

IF I BECOME ONE WITH SINBAD, I CAN RETURN TO THE EARTH! I'M *CERTAIN* A DIMENSIONAL HOLE WILL OPEN! I JUST KNOW IT! WA HA HA HA!!

THE DAVID WHO WAS SOLOMON'S LONG-LIVED FATHER AND THE EVIL MAGICIAN OF ALMA TRAN!

WHAT DO YOU MEAN?

OH, YOU KNOW HIM! HE WAS HERE, BUT THEN RETURNED TO LIFE.

THE PEOPLE WHO DIED IN ALMA TRAN TURNED INTO BLACK RUKH AND RETURNED TO IL-IRRAH. DAVID DID TOO, SO HE WAS HERE WITH US.

I...

...WASN'T READY TO DIE!

TH-THERE MUST BE SOME WAY TO GET BACK!!

ACTUALLY, ONE PERSON DID LEAVE AND RETURN TO LIFE.

HE WAS AN EXCEPTION.

HE RETURNED TO LIFE?!

SO I'M REALLY DEAD?

PROBABLY NOT HERE. YOU DON'T APPEAR TO BE FROM ALMA TRAN.

IS THIS THE AFTERLIFE? WHERE ARE MY PARENTS?

YEAH!

I *DIED?!* RIGHT IN THE MIDDLE OF EVERYTHING?!

UH-HUH. AND YOU CAN'T LEAVE. NO ONE EVER HAS.

I WAS DEAD FOR A LITTLE WHILE AND GOT THROWN INTO A STRANGE SPACE. AT FIRST, I WAS TOTALLY CONFUSED.

HUH? WASN'T I JUST FIGHTING HAKURYU?

Night 344:
Laying the Foundation

BUT YOU'RE DEAD NOW, SO IT DOESN'T MATTER.

WHERE'D YOU COME FROM, BOY?

THEY LOOK LIKE THE PEOPLE FROM ALMA TRAN THAT ALADDIN SHOWED US.

LOOKING AT THEIR FACES, I REALIZED SOMETHING.

I CAN'T LEAVE?!

AND YOU CAN NEVER LEAVE.

YOU'RE PART OF IL-IRRAH NOW.

WHEN I DIRECTED MY ATTENTION TOWARD OTHERS, I WAS SURPRISED. MANY PEOPLE APPEARED ALL AROUND ME.

WAHID, HE JUST DIED, SO HIS MEMORIES ARE FRESH AND VIVID.

ALL THAT CLATTER BUGS ME!

NO WAY! YOUR MEMORIES ARE *OBSESSED* WITH THOSE THINGS, SO YOU'RE STILL ATTACHED TO THEM!

BUT *OUR* APPETITES FOR SEX AND FOOD ARE GONE, SETTA.

OH... I AM?

JOLT

OR RATHER, THEY HAD BEEN THERE FROM THE BEGINNING.

WHO ARE YOU? WHERE DID YOU COME FROM?

90

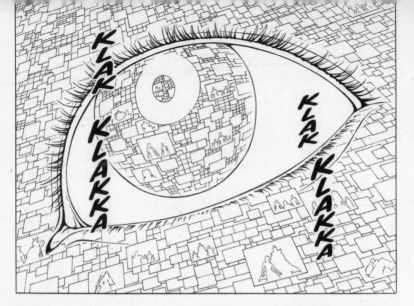

THEN I WONDERED WHAT EVERYONE ELSE WAS DOING.

I WATCHED THOUSANDS OF TIMES...

...AND REALIZED I HAD NEVER ACHIEVED ANYTHING.

LOOKS LIKE THERE'S A LIVELY NEW ARRIVAL!

AW, NOW I'M DEAD.

THE REALIZATION WELLED WITHIN ME.

?

MY MEMORIES FROM LIFE... REPEATING... ENDLESSLY.

I SAT THERE STARING AS THEY PASSED BEFORE ME.

THEN I SAW MEMORIES OF MY LIFE PLAYING ON AND ON.

CLAK

CLAK

ALL RIGHT...

...BUT I DIDN'T GO BECAUSE I *WANTED* TO.

I LOST A FIGHT TO HAKURYU IN RAKUSHO AND FELL UNCONSCIOUS.

IT WAS STRANGE. IT WAS NEITHER HOT NOR COLD, AND NO ONE WAS THERE.

THE NEXT THING I KNEW, I WAS IN AN OPEN SPACE.

...

I JUST WANT THIS TO *END*.

TMP TMP

...

OH... YOU DID?

UM... I MET SOME ACQUAIN-TANCES OF YOURS.

YEAH! SETTA AND WAHID!

WHAT ARE YOU TALKING ABOUT?

SEE IF YOU AND ALIBABA CAN STOP ME!

IS THAT THE FOURTH DUNGEON?

DUNGEON NO. 4
THE TRIAL OF INSANITY AND GLOOM
FURFUR

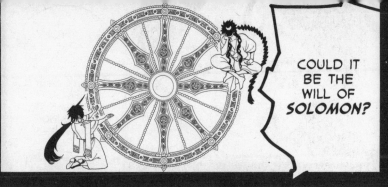

COULD IT BE THE WILL OF **SOLOMON?**

HOW PRESUMPTUOUS OF YOU TO CRITICIZE ME WITH YOUR *TRIFLING* MORALITY!

OR MAYBE SOMEONE EVEN HIGHER THAN KING SOLOMON IS RAISING ME UP AS DIVINE!

SILENCE

TEE HEE

Night 343:
A Certain Space

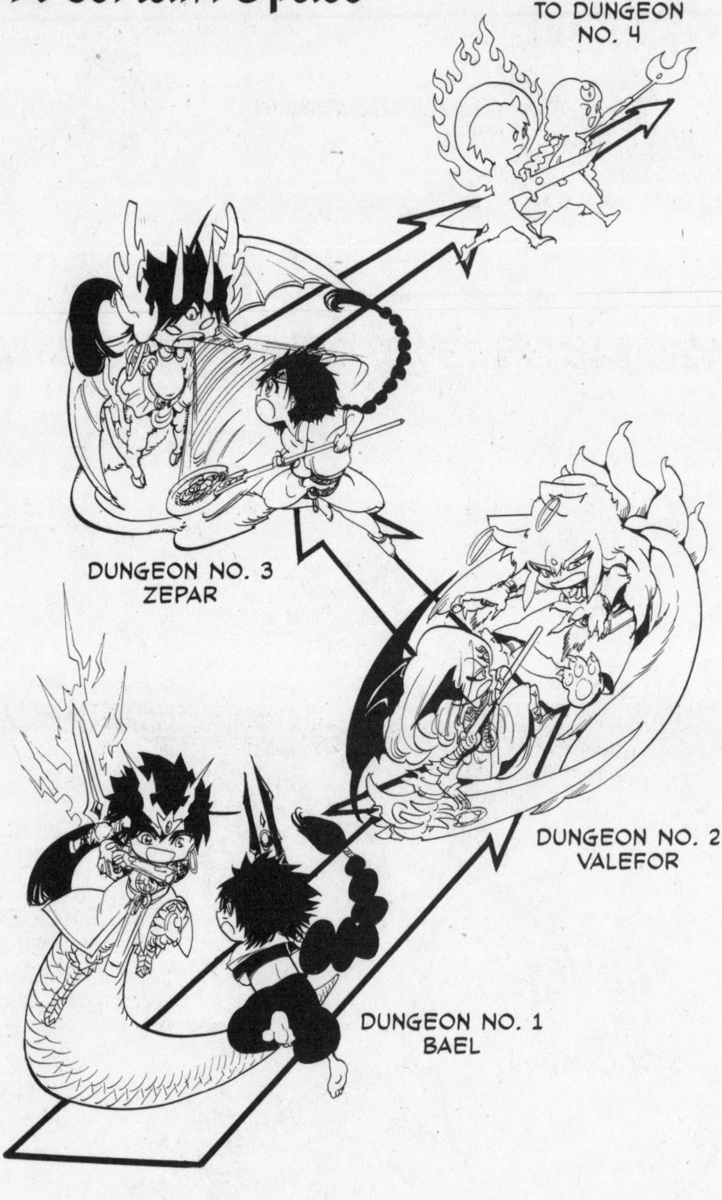

TO DUNGEON
NO. 4

DUNGEON NO. 3
ZEPAR

DUNGEON NO. 2
VALEFOR

DUNGEON NO. 1
BAEL

HOW SAD...

...

BECAUSE AS LONG AS HUMAN BEINGS LIVE LIKE HUMAN BEINGS, WAR AND INJUSTICE WILL NEVER CHANGE, NO MATTER HOW MANY TIMES YOU REFORMULATE THE WORLD.

YOU JUST FEEL *SAD.*

I FINALLY UNDER-STAND.

Hurry!!

Calm down...

THE SUN IS SINK-ING.

BUT...

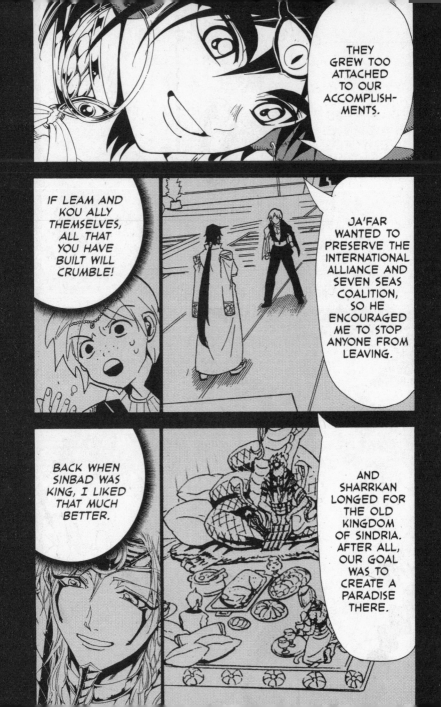

NONETHELESS, NO ONE WANTS THE WORLD TO CHANGE. EVEN MY FORMER COMRADES DIDN'T WANT ME TO BE SO REVOLUTIONARY.

NOTHING IS WORSE THAN GOING NOWHERE AND NEVER CHANGING.

YOU'RE RIGHT, ALADDIN.

FORMER COMRADES? LIKE WHO?

?

THE EIGHT GENERALS!

WHAT ARE YOU *THINK-ING?!*

DO THEY MEAN MORE THAN YOUR *FRIENDS?*

...

...BUT YOU AND I CAN DISCUSS THIS!

I'VE NEVER BEEN ABLE TO DISCUSS THE SACRED PALACE AND HUMAN EVOLUTION...

MEETING PEOPLE MAKES US *EVOLVE,* HUH?

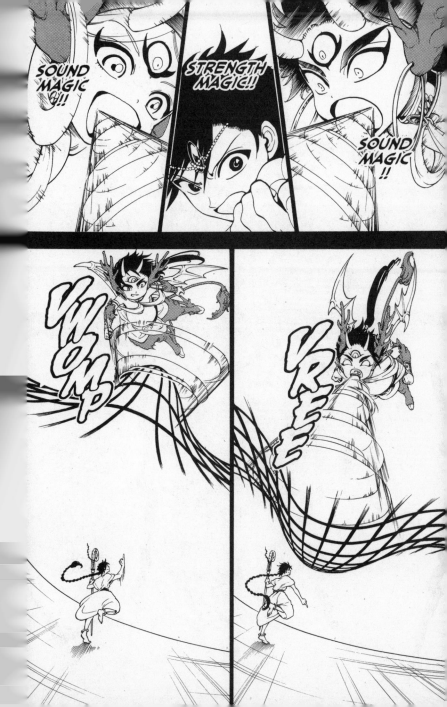

THIS WOMAN WAS A PARTEBIAN PRINCESS.

HER NAME IS SERENDINE!

I BOUGHT A NATION FROM THE PARTEBIAN EMPIRE AND TRIED TO ESTABLISH MY FIRST KINGDOM.

AT THAT TIME, I WAS TRYING TO OBTAIN MY OWN COUNTRY.

WELCOME! ZEPAR IS THE DUNGEON I CAPTURED AT AGE 17!

PARTEBIAN PRINCESS?

SO...

SHE WAS THE DJINN ZEPAR'S FIRST MASTER.

IT'S SINBAD AND... WHO IS THAT?

DUNGEON NO. 3
THE TRIAL OF
SPIRIT AND CONTROL
ZEPAR

I CAN SEE
SOMETHING!

...HIS GOAL ISN'T TO HAVE US PERSUADE HIM?

IS HE AFTER SOMETHING ELSE?!

WE'VE ARRIVED! THIS IS THE THIRD DUNGEON!

HE BECAME A GOD, BUT WHEN HE REWROTE THE RUKH, IT DIDN'T AFFECT *US*.

AND THAT'S HOLDING HIM BACK.

IT WAS LIKE HE'D BEEN WAITING!

...THAT SOMEONE COULD CHALLENGE HIM.

AND WHEN HE FOUND OUT, HE SEEMED HAPPY...

MY WILL CANNOT REACH YOU.

ALI-BABA, YOU ARE UN-USUAL.

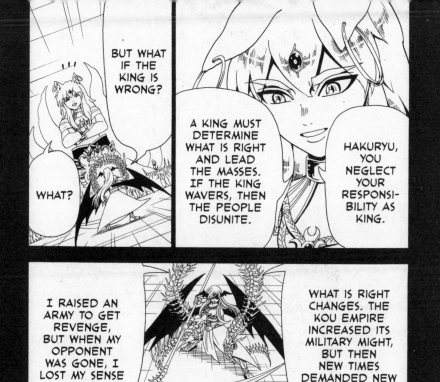

BUT WHAT IF THE KING IS WRONG?

A KING MUST DETERMINE WHAT IS RIGHT AND LEAD THE MASSES. IF THE KING WAVERS, THEN THE PEOPLE DISUNITE.

WHAT?

HAKURYU, YOU NEGLECT YOUR RESPONSIBILITY AS KING.

I RAISED AN ARMY TO GET REVENGE, BUT WHEN MY OPPONENT WAS GONE, I LOST MY SENSE OF SELF.

WHAT IS RIGHT CHANGES. THE KOU EMPIRE INCREASED ITS MILITARY MIGHT, BUT THEN NEW TIMES DEMANDED NEW METHODS.

...

AND WHAT ABOUT *YOU?*

Night 340:
A Decisive Battle

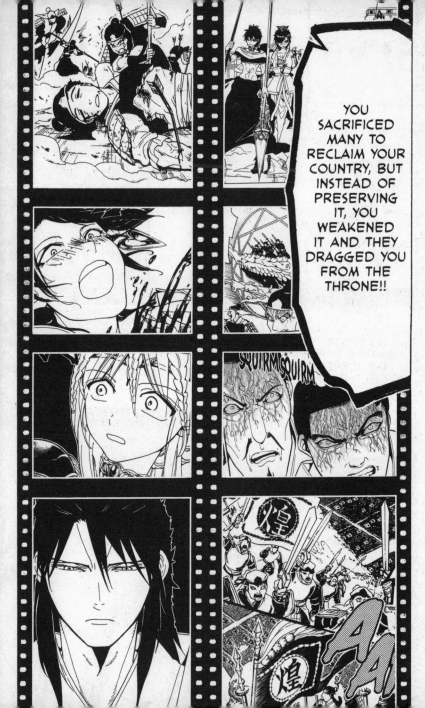

Night 339:
The Creed of
Falsehood and Faith

MAGI
The labyrinth of magic

35

CONTENTS

MAGI
The labyrinth of magic

35

Story & Art by
SHINOBU OHTAKA